Profiles in Persuasion

How to Stand Up, Stay Credible, and Win People Over in a Deeply Divided World

Peter Afrasiabi

CONTENTS

Introduction

"All my efforts are always concerned with this goal—for I will say it again and again—to do some good by my speaking, if I can, and if not, at least to do no harm."

—MARCUS TULLIUS CICERO, *ON THE IDEAL ORATOR*, 55 BCE[1]

They were a most unlikely pair. One had written a famed song "Pride (In the Name of Love)" that eulogized Martin Luther King, Jr.; the other had attempted to stop the United States Senate from creating a national holiday in honor of Martin Luther King, Jr. The first, U2's frontman, Bono, was a liberal rock star from Europe who often wore black leather jackets and wraparound sunglasses indoors, a man whose lyrics often challenged government abuses while he used his rock star fame to fight for liberal causes for decades. The second was Senator Jesse Helms, a deeply conservative, religious senator from North Carolina, part of the World War II generation, a man who had once loudly opposed the racial integration of public schools in the South. But in 2002, they found themselves together in an old, dark office in Washington, D.C., where Bono set out to persuade Senator Helms to drop his long-standing, rigid philosophical opposition to a congressional AIDS relief bill. The odds were heavily stacked against Bono. The meeting ended with Senator Helms crying. What transpired in that short, tense meeting? As we will unpackage shortly, Bono successfully *persuaded* by employing specific, learnable persuasion tools to please, prove, and then move Senator Helms to his viewpoint.

In truth, we all are engaged in persuasion every day in all aspects of our lives. How so? Because we stand up for ourselves, for our children; we stand up for issues and points of view we believe in; we stand up for our companies and employers in selling their services and products; sometimes we want to stand up but are paralyzed by indecision in what to say; and sometimes we stand up when forced by life's circumstances. And each time, at that exact moment, we are engaged in persuasion.

This book therefore profiles five stories of true successful persuasion efforts by individuals convincing others to join them; arguing for a viewpoint they believe is correct; winning over their skeptical audience with positive, respectful words; finding common ground amidst enemies; overcoming staggering odds; and inspiring and moving others to new heights, all through effective persuasion techniques. All our stories are ones where the outcome of the issue subject to persuasion was far from certain, in fact where it was stacked against the person who prevailed. But the victor overcame the odds for two specific reasons: first, because persuasion tools were employed properly, and second, because they did not adopt false conceptions of persuasion tools. These stories then are a window into the inner workings of persuasion at work in the real world, and they allow us to explore and learn the tools of persuasion, so that we all can be more successful communicators for our beliefs and positions. And the truth is that effective persuasion is learnable by any of us as you will see as we work through the stories to fill our persuasion toolbox with the tools of persuasion.

But before we explore our five stories of persuasion to give you these persuasion tools, let's start with an immediate story, a real one, of two similarly situated employees, Jackie and Diane. Both Jackie and Diane (fictitious names used here) were employed by my law firm, and both asked my law firm for a large raise at the same time. Both had almost identical jobs. Both wanted to stand up for themselves. But their efforts to persuade us of their need for a raise took two very different paths.

Jackie wanted a large raise, almost 30 percent, and approached us with data from other companies showing what they paid for her job position. She explained that the market price was in the data she provided us and said that she was entitled to that amount to be compensated fairly.

Diane wanted a raise also, almost the same large percentage amount. But Diane told us a different story. She shared with us her work over the last year and how she had helped make sure we kept deadlines, how she had worked late to make sure we filed documents timely, and how she had been a team player within the company to protect certain clients when we had specific difficult times in particular cases. She shared those events that had occurred over the prior year.

Jackie's data was not fake data, and Diane's stories of what she did for our business were also true. Jackie and Diane each presented reasons, or arguments, for a raise. But notice how the arguments—their stories—differ. Jackie's argument was that the market said we were underpaying her, and so, at a subtle level, her pitch was that she was being treated unfairly by us and that she had already in fact been shortchanged by us. That argument, even assuming her data perfectly appropriate and accurate, was an effort at proving a string of logic through a story to cause us to act: I am underpaid, the market data proves it, I have been historically shortchanged, you took that benefit from me, thus you should give me the raise. Diane's pitch to us involved a different story: I love being part of this team, I have made the enterprise better, I would like a raise for my contribution and efforts.

Diane stood up for herself and persuaded us; Jackie stood up for herself and did not persuade us. Why? Answering why Diane's approach worked and Jackie's failed takes us to the inner workings of persuasion. Diane used multiple of our tools of persuasion successfully—she told a compelling *story* to move us, she offered careful and accurate logic, and she stood as an authentic voice for her request. On the other hand, Jackie's story lacked any narrative structure and was a negative one of aggrievement that set us apart from her instead of bringing us together and, as we'll explore later, was based on faulty logic.

That's just part of the persuasion issues we can distill from Jackie's and Diane's approaches as a means to explore the tools of persuasion, so don't forget about Jackie and Diane as we will come back to them at various points while we explore our profile stories to show where that persuasion exercise by these two people, all at the same time, worked for one but failed for the other.

Persuasion: Pleasing, Proving, and Moving

Learning to persuade someone to your viewpoint involves the learnable three-fold practice of pleasing, proving, and moving someone else through your words as the medium of communicating your message. Pleasing requires us to be a speaker who commands the respect of the audience so that the specific audience (friend, boss, team, social group, coworker, etc.) is receptive to hearing the message. This has two principal elements: credibility and authenticity/honesty. Proving involves the internal logic and story chosen to justify the persuasion effort and request of the audience. Moving involves the use of the right emotion and spoken or written words to convince the audience to agree with you as articulated through your story. These base definitions will take on richer and deeper meaning, with tangible lessons for everyday use, as we work through the five profiles in persuasion. In short, if you think of persuasion as a stool, then the three legs that hold up the stool are the pleasing, proving, and moving legs of the stool.

The Persuasion Stool. Like the three legs of a stool that are needed to hold up the stool and the weight of the person, persuasion is based on three critical principles, each of which is related and necessary to perform the function of persuasion well.

These three principles of pleasing, proving, and moving find ancient and modern refuge. History's greatest ancient orator and advocate Marcus Tullius Cicero built on Aristotle's rhetorical ideas of ethos, logos, and pathos, and reformulated Aristotle's three concepts. Cicero wrote that the ideal orator "is the one whose speech instructs, delights, and moves the minds of his audience."[2] Cicero's "delights" was Aristotle's ethos (today: please), his "instructs" was Aristotle's logos (today: prove), and his "moves the minds" was Aristotle's pathos (today: move). Aristotle's and Cicero's construct is what we can again reformulate for our time and world, and hence the terms "*please, prove,* and *move*." Today, how do we connect with our audience to please, prove, and move, and thus successfully persuade? With the multiple tools of persuasion—some tools relating to pleasing, others to proving, and still others to moving—that our profile stories in this book distill.

Persuasion cuts through every aspect of our collective and coordinated community living experience, precisely because we all exist in multiple groups—work environments, corporate boardrooms, family, friends, city, yoga or gym studio, national body politic, and more—and we mediate those existences, and the disagreements that exist in them, through communication. Unless we all understand how persuasion works—how the act of communicating and articulating your position and confronting different positions in a manner that can best persuade another to your position and thus best be able to persuade one to your viewpoint—we will continue to find ourselves in often angry and polarized strife, not reaching the outcome we hoped for.

Why This Book Matters Now

Words have vibrations, good and bad. Too often in the modern world, we see debating politicians or community members, friends, and even family, often in social media, all of whom do immense harm with their words, all in efforts at persuading others to their viewpoint. And we regularly see *both* the winner and loser of an issue do harm with words, and so a core persuasion principle is missed by both the winner and loser. This matters because both will need to engage again one day. Those word vibrations matter, and effective persuasion concerns itself with not just the positive word vibrations, but also the damage done to your future credibility and ability to stand up for yourself by often-unintended negative word vibrations.

Why now? Why this book? More than ever, we have—through social media and the modern media world at large—created echo chambers of short interactions and blusterous speech, written or oral, racing to reach outcomes and often demonizing those who disagree with us, all couched ostensibly in terms of communication aimed at persuading others. In so many aspects of our collective social discourse, there are now two viewpoints, one right, one wrong, and each convinced they are right and the other wrong. This gulf between people on micro and macro levels is itself emblematic of the fact that successful persuasion techniques are not being actively deployed. For when successful efforts at persuasion are employed, two people on different sides of an issue can each see the other side and embrace the genuine reasonableness that can inhabit each side's point of view: One wins, one loses on the narrow persuasion exercise, but *both* also win, and they can leave friends and respectful of the other, not ruled by bitter hatred and tension, instead each understanding and respecting that contrary viewpoints can each be persuasive. It's why our lead story is of two people who are at first blush polar opposites: a liberal rock star who rose to worldwide celebrity in the 1980s singing against modern political systems and a highly conservative North Carolina senator from the World War II generation who epitomized a powerful government institutionalist. When we unpackage carefully how persuasion works, we can see how proper persuasion can bring even those seemingly light-years apart closer together.

Positive Persuasion Techniques: It's About More Than Just Winning

Many of the lessons this book explores through its stories are lessons some of us learn over many years of life's hard knocks, even if we do not conceptualize them in the "persuasion" terms we explore here. But all of us—to manage a staff, effectively get that raise, deal with the angry school principal, secure that promotion, sell that product or service, be a successful leader in an organization—need to recognize that we all are, and must be, persuasive advocates. Through the stories here, we break down what persuasion is—where, why, and how it works, and, critically, where, why, and how it fails—so that when you stand up for yourself, a family member, an administrator at a school and have to speak to constituents about a new program. You are a service professional with younger team members you must motivate and move along. The real-world examples are endless, and at some point, we all have to move others in such one-on-many structures.

Still others are what we can label one-versus-one situations where you compete against someone to get a third party to decide who prevails. Here, one example we will look at involves the fascinating story of ancient Rome's Symmachus and Ambrose, each pitting their persuasion tools against the other, each trying to convince the Roman Emperor to either keep the Altar of Victory in the Roman Senate or remove it as an affront to the growing Christian Church. This is no different from your having to compete against a coworker to justify an executive's decision to pick one project over another. Or when you compete against another company to land a contract. Or when you pitch for work for your company against competitors. In each, your persuasive efforts are competing against another's persuasive efforts in front of a higher power that decides a winner and loser.

The Central Role of Stories in Successful Persuasion

Finally, *stories* matter to ponder the persuasion lessons, because a book of prescriptions has no meaning or application outside of context. Stories—the ones we tell friends and family, the ones we read, and the ones we watch in movies and episodic television—are a critical cornerstone to successful persuasion, so what better way to explore persuasion than by looking at stories of successful persuasion. By approaching our subject here through *stories*—actual profile stories of persuasion at work—rather than a checklist of prescriptions, we can understand why they worked, what would have happened with different approaches, and how then, distilling and discussing the specific persuasion tools from these stories, we may all find better ways to communicate effectively our beliefs, positions, arguments, and ideas so that we may please, prove, and move another to a viewpoint.

Not one of our five stories covers every aspect of persuasion's pleasing, proving, and moving goals, but across the five stories, we are able to explore the different tools in the persuasion toolbox so that, upon assessing all our stories, all the various aspects of positive persuasion are illuminated in practical, learnable terms, so that we all may employ them as we stand up for our positions. And at the end of this book, so that you may keep in mind the lessons from our profiles in persuasion stories, there is a summary chart of the tools learned through the stories that can act as a handy reference for you as you go forth and persuade, standing up for your beliefs and needs.

CHAPTER 1

U2's Bono and North Carolina Senator Jesse Helms

"When the conduct of men is designed to be influenced, persuasion, kind, unassuming persuasion, should ever be adopted. It is an old and a true maxim, that a 'drop of honey catches more flies than a gallon of gall.'"

—ABRAHAM LINCOLN, TEMPERANCE ADDRESS AT SPRINGFIELD, FEBRUARY 22, 1842

The Meeting

It's probably an understatement to say they were an unlikely pair. Bono came from Ireland, born in Dublin in 1960 as Paul David Hewson as part of the baby boomer generation, and with his band members formed their band while in high school as teenagers in the late 1970s. Bono and U2 shot to worldwide fame and stardom in the 1980s, singing, at times, protest songs against government oppression. At the Live Aid concert in London in 1985, Bono famously left the stage and danced with one of the 72,000 attendees; while at the same concert, he sang his famous "Sunday Bloody Sunday" song, where the lyrics addressed the British government's

of America Tour," where he traveled to various cities, spoke about the AIDS crisis in Africa that he had witnessed firsthand on his travels, played some songs, and argued for change. This journey led him to be involved publicly in working to get AIDS relief money to Africa. Thus, by 2002, Bono and many others had been arguing publicly for several years for larger programs and passage of the law.

As you can see, the roadblock to getting the bill passed was Senator Helms. This is what brings us to a most remarkable story of persuasion that pits Bono's beliefs and positions against Senator Helms's beliefs and positions. What on earth, you ask, could cause these two men to have anything in common to even justify their sitting down and talking?

There was one thing: religion. Senator Helms is not the only Christian in our story; Bono is too and has never been shy about being a famous rock star and also a Christian. Famously, after U2 released its first album and the band members were starting their journey into rock stardom, the band questioned whether the life of a rock band was consistent with their Christian beliefs as some members, Bono included, considered ending the nascent band.[6] While a scant few of U2's many hundreds of songs expressly touch on Christianity, Bono does not shy away from his Christian faith and its influence on his identity where he openly touches on it in his music, through religious imagery and words at concerts, and his writings.

Here is one of many possible examples to consider. In 2001—the same time period when Bono was working on the AIDS relief program—during U2's live musical performances on their worldwide "Elevation Tour," in the musical bridge phase between the immensely popular songs "Bad" and "Where the Streets Have No Name," as the first song phases into the second song and the crowd is screaming and cheering, Bono offers a chant, his version of Psalm 116:12-13, while the slow and anthemic build of the musical progression of "Where the Streets Have No Name" builds to its climax and the beginning of the lyrics.

In this bridge, Bono impromptu sings, "What can I give back to God for the blessings He has poured out on me? What can I give back to God for the blessings He has poured out on me? I lift high the cup of salvation, it is a toast to our Father, follow through on a promise I made to you, from the heart." He ends his rendition of the Psalm with a genuinely raw, guttural, and powerful emotional cry to the heavens, as the iconic song then erupts in its early climactic familiar musical form, and the crowd excitedly screams and pulsates throughout the stadium. Watching and listening to it can only give justice to the moving nature of the event and the open badge of faith Bono willingly wears, riffing on the Psalm as a powerful building backdrop to perhaps the band's most anthemic stadium song.[7]

So, Senator Helms agreed to talk to Bono. Bono arrived at the Capitol, wearing his trademark wraparound glasses, albeit not in his leather outfits seen on the U2 concert stage. Bono made his way through the labyrinthine Senate building hallways and arrived at Senator Helms's old office, where Senator Helms, dressed in his standard Washington, D.C., conservative suit and power red tie, awaited the rock star in his large office with walls adorned with photos of famed people he had met over the decades.

Inside the office, the men sat down together. Bono started by quoting the Gospel of Matthew from the Bible.[8] In the Gospel of Matthew 25:31-46, Jesus talks of a final judgment of humankind where people are separated based upon how they lived their life treating the less fortunate. Two groups are made, sheep and goats, and the ultimate question will be whether on earth a person served those most in need—the sick, the poor, all strangers.[9]

Bono also offered, in modern political terms, "This is not a conservative or liberal issue, but it's an issue impacting children. There are ten million orphans created by the disease. We can prevent ten million more children from losing their parents and from contracting the disease themselves." Senator Helms just listened.[10]

For his story, Bono again turned to the Bible and discussed the parable of Jesus and leprosy in the ancient world.[11] This biblical story from the Gospels involves various interactions Jesus had with lepers. In the first chapter of Mark's Gospel, a leper asks Jesus to heal him. And Jesus touches the leper to heal the sick man. Jesus does not turn away or refuse to touch him for fear of the disease. This, notwithstanding the fact that in the Old Testament laws in Leviticus (13-14), those with leprosy were affirmatively ostracized.

Basically, Bono's story posited, leprosy was a feared contagious disease in the ancient world. Those with leprosy were treated in their time as societal outcasts. Jesus taught that they needed compassion, and even physical touching, despite perceived societal risks of the time; Jesus taught that compassion for the sick must reign supreme. And in the modern world, AIDS victims were innocents also and should be treated as Christ demanded we treat lepers in the ancient world, not with disdain, discrimination, and distance, but with compassion and love.

Bono thus asked, "How could addressing the disease not be at the center of Christ's mission?"[12]

Silence, no doubt, hung heavily in the air.

And then Senator Helms broke down in tears.

"Son, I want to bless you," Helms told Bono. "Let me put my hands on you."[13]

And so, Senator Helms, the once steadfast opponent of the AIDS relief bill, was crying and, remarkably, actively blessing Bono.

"I'm so ashamed that I have done so little," Senator Helms even said later, ashamed that he had not done more to address the AIDS pandemic.[14] "I have always been an advocate of a very limited government, particularly as it concerns overseas commitments. ... We also have a higher calling, and in the end, our conscience is answerable to God."[15]

In that office in the Capitol, Senator Helms had changed his viewpoint. But Senator Helms did not just cease his opposition to the pending bill. He remarkably and affirmatively became a co-sponsor of the bill, lobbying others for its passage. In 2003, the bill passed through Congress, and President Bush signed it into law. In Congress, when President Bush gave a speech about it, he even smiled and remarked that, "Dick Cheney came into the Oval Office and said, 'Jesse Helms wants you to listen to Bono.'"[16]

The bill passed, and massive financial relief flowed to Africa to help manage the AIDS crisis that was still ravaging the continent, and world, in the early twenty-first century.

Since 2003 when the bill passed, twenty-six million lives have been saved, and eight million babies have been saved from being born with HIV.[17]

Let's now unpackage this story to see it in persuasion's terms to start developing our persuasion toolbox.

U2's Bono and Senator Helms. Public domain image from the United States government.

because it demonstrates that identifying an argument (i.e., Helms is arguably not following the teachings of the Bible) is just not enough; it must be an argument that you as a speaker can *credibly* deliver. For the given point you want to make or argument you want to press to justify your position—a promotion, a raise, a corporate contract, assistance from a teacher for your child in some setting—you need to meet both of these aspects of credibility-based pleasing to successfully persuade your audience. If your contemplated approach does not satisfy both elements, then you will not be able to please in your efforts despite the apparent logic of your argument.

Let's take this to our daily lives. Imagine a basic situation as follows: A teacher is not giving enough help in the classroom to your child who has hyperactivity and instead, you feel, sees the child as a problem child. You are a parent, but you are not a professional educator. Let's assume you go to the teacher and tell the teacher that her teaching style does not work for your child, and she needs to be less negative to your child. Do you have your multiple levels of credibility? You are not a teacher, you have not taught students for decades, you have not managed hyperactive children in classes for decades, but the teacher has. You thus do not have the first-level credibility to please the teacher with your argument and will have the audience immediately skeptical of the argument that you are advocating for. But what if you change your approach? What if you start by discussing how for specific behavioral issues in the home, you have found that a specific approach works really well to keep the disruptive hyperactive behavior down? Now you have expertise in solving that specific problem—based on your firsthand experience—and the teacher will be more likely to be receptive to your argument because, on that approach, you are credible. You also have authenticity and honesty because you are sharing the problem and solution you have explored yourself in your parenting struggles, and you are not taking a position of superiority as it relates to educational knowledge over the teacher, which, because you lack such superiority from a traditional expertise basis, otherwise causes your entire approach to lack the basic kind of honesty needed to get people to meet you at your argument.

Or let us return to Jackie and Diane. When Jackie said that others earned nearly 30 percent more so she should too, it would have been the identical approach to Bono's sitting down in Senator Helms's office and telling Senator Helms that he should support the bill because his foreign policy ideas were wrong and because many other leaders supported the aid. Jackie spoke to people who run the firm and know how much money it has, what its finances are, and what it can afford. The people running the firm also know very well what similar firms pay similar employees, so it is much harder to convince experts in an area that they are wrong. Jackie lacked the credibility to deliver the economic message that her specific job in this specific industry was 30 percent off market in pay (it turns out she did lack the knowledge as her data was, if not apples to oranges, Fuji apples to Granny Smith apples, which we will return to later). This left Jackie lacking credibility, and, as a result, she could not begin to please her audience with her efforts at persuasion.

Your Audience: Know Them and Respect Them

Pleasing and being able then to move the audience is a function of whom you are speaking to, that is, your audience. It is always the case that in order to try to persuade a person or a group of people, you have to know exactly whom they are and how they operate and what they value in their operating systems, so you may develop the right credibility with them. Bono understood Senator Helms as a conservative Christian senator, a man of deep faith. Bono knew he had to establish credibility with that person—that specific audience—to deliver his persuasive efforts. This requires spending time to understand the motivations and basis for the positions of those you are advocating with. Bono did this by discussing the

Gospels immediately with Senator Helms, an area of common ground for both men.

A critical part of the credibility you build is by also respecting the voice of the other side. Let's pivot again to how Bono would have fared if he had not approached Senator Helms with a healthy sense of respect for the man and his beliefs. For example, if Bono had approached his meeting with an intention to argue that Senator Helms was wrong on American foreign policy, he would not have been able to persuade. After all, Senator Helms may well be interested at some level in what a European rock star thinks about the proper exercise of American foreign policy, but it is hard to see how a long-term senator and head of the Senate Foreign Relations Committee would believe that a foreign rock star is more intelligent on the nuances of American foreign policy than a sitting American senator (domestic long-term senators from both sides of the aisle, after all, were not able to convince Senator Helms).

In all persuasion efforts, there is much gray, and rarely is it purely black and white. This requires one to recognize that you must be able to respect the fact that reasonable minds can differ on an immense amount of our human issues and disagreements. The act of humility toward your position translates to respecting the fact that someone who is a polar opposite can in fact hold a contrary belief in good faith. Once understood and employed, you can then identify common ground and reach out to someone from a playing field of respect. This demonstrates your openness to flexibility and also the fact that you do not hold the other side in contempt. This is exactly how bridges are built. Here, Bono achieved exactly this by not lecturing Senator Helms that he was wrong on political policy as it relates to foreign aid, and instead, as a result, by necessarily respecting Senator Helms's political policy beliefs. Respected on political philosophy grounds, Senator Helms was amenable to listening to Bono's message as framed through a joint shared lens of core Christian values.

Properly pleasing and then being able to move your audience requires, thus, success at an additional layer: humility for your position and respect for the reasonableness of counter positions to your beliefs. In this sense, Bono embodied Abraham Lincoln's "drop of honey" quote this chapter opened with, and by employing this approach, he avoided the wrong story and settled on the more persuasive story.

Back to Jackie and Diane. Jackie's persuasion effort offered only data and her only story was that she was underpaid, that she was being treated unfairly as a result compared to other companies, and, implicitly, that we had treated her unfairly in this respect for some time. That is a heavy charge that demonstrates that we the employers were held in a level of contempt by our own employee, and such a charge does not even permit the employer to defend the salary, for if someone indicates such alleged mistreatment in that way, it is hard to conceptualize how to bridge the gap—after all, we could not tell her that we could afford only a 5 percent raise for she has already made clear that absent 30 percent more, she is in a position of mistreatment. This, then, is the issue of not understanding your audience and finding common ground with them. If Jackie thought she was starting high to settle low and get a smaller raise, the method backfired. Diane, on the other hand, approached us with an explanation of her successes and contributions to the firm as the vehicle to ask for a raise, and that allowed for common ground over her teamwork and contribution, even if we could not afford the full raise. Diane, like Bono, knew the audience; Jackie missed the audience.

All too often, however, logic is the beginning and often the end point of persuasion efforts by people. Too much weight is placed on the idea that if you can present something that is "logical," the other side will change their position and agree. In this sense, far too much weight is placed on logic, as if it were the beginning and end of the persuasion exercise. Instead, logic functions as an important part of persuasion, but it must fit within the broader framework of an appropriate story to employ whatever logic you are utilizing. And, by starting and depending solely upon logic in your persuasion effort, you imply that the other person is not logical (a character challenge) or that another outcome would defy other versions of logic. This last point is important, as there is not a sacrosanct, inviolable set of "logic" that all people accept or buy into: People may reject the version or weight of the deductive or inductive logic you use, belief systems and human experiences can render your chosen logic less persuasive, one's truths are not another's truths, and so "logic" alone is not capable of simply proving your goal. The brilliant physicist Niels Bohr reportedly captured this idea when he noted that the opposite of a profound truth may well be another profound truth.[19]

Bono, thus, used the logic of reasoning by analogy to similar situations within the context of a broader story that could move his audience, a story not dependent on only root logic. Bono was essentially arguing that Jesus taught that people in the ancient world with terrible diseases, who were discriminated against and shunned from ancient society, should have instead been loved and helped; that was part of the revolution of Jesus's message for the world. Likewise today, there are sick people in the modern world who are discriminated against and shunned from society and are not receiving help. Therefore, to truly follow in the path of Jesus Christ, a Christian should be willing to help people today the way Jesus helped people in his age. At its core, that is nothing more than reasoning by analogy within basic logic. But Bono had a story to deliver that logic: the story of Jesus and the lepers to illuminate the core role of charity in Christianity that Senator Helms and he shared as a belief set.

Now, imagine if Bono had chosen a different story. Certainly, he could have built a story to make the pitch for AIDS relief around the tragic experience of a child with AIDS in Africa. He could have told a compelling, heart-wrenching story in that fashion using an actual child (photograph and all) and the suffering of that child in his community in Africa. But how would his audience have responded to that story? Senator Helms would have heard such a tragic story, and his response would probably have been that, while his heart breaks for the suffering, there are equal stories of suffering here in the United States with American children in need of help. And then Senator Helms's rebuttal story would have supported his first-level approach to the issue: Political philosophy about helping people in the United States first before other countries should be the governing framework. And Bono also would have missed his audience with that story as it could have potentially implied that the child's death was somehow Senator Helms's fault or belonged on his moral conscience. Thus, the wrong story could boomerang and provoke in the listener a retrenchment to their starting position, thereby leading you to fail in your persuasion exercise. This is why it is not just that you pick a story; it is that you carefully and intentionally pick the right story given the other pieces of the persuasion puzzle we are addressing here.

Let's turn back to Jackie and Diane and see this story aspect of persuasion at work. Diane had a story that could connect with her audience, one of participating in a team to help the firm's client in hard times, a story that demonstrated her commitment to the firm, passion for the firm's clients, and unwavering willingness to help—work she always did in the moment quietly but happily to better the whole enterprise. But Jackie had no such story and had instead data that served only a logical purpose (others get paid $X; therefore, so should I). In this sense, Jackie was stuck with root logic that had surface appeal (let's assume her logic was correct, for now), the same way people had approached Senator Helms with data about the AIDS crisis, but Jackie failed in persuasion because she did not fit that logic and data into a broader story that could appeal to her audience. Because Jackie's story was tethered only to the asserted logic of a raise driven by data comparisons to others, her story necessarily implied that we were bad actors (we had severely underpaid her for years and so were exploitive), a charge people are obviously very reluctant to agree with. Jackie's story thus failed. In our next chapter, we will dive deeply into the building blocks of stories and how to craft them.

Put-downs or Character Attacks Damage Persuasion Efforts

One of the most important parts of persuasion that we repeatedly see in the modern world—whether it is in private discourse between people; online debating of ideas or issues in social media; politicians from the highest level down to the local level; or friends and family when they sit around and engage in debate over how to raise children, correct behavior, or decide where to move to a new home—is the use of negative character attacks or put-downs against the person they are trying to persuade. In an effort to win an argument, people reflexively decide to impugn the character of the other speaker, and thereby use that to show that they have superiority, and the other person is morally culpable in some fashion. And this is where the cardinal rule of Cicero quoted at the outset is again tripped, for it leads to doing harm with your words for which there is no persuasion benefit.

Negativity and character attacks fail for fundamental persuasion reasons. First, casting negative aspersions on someone else's character rather than taking the high road damages your ability to persuade. This is known in formal persuasion terms as going "ad hominem" (Latin for "aimed at the man") as a means of attacking their character rather than their argument. It is a logical fallacy that people employ to distract, but if you employ it, then you damage your persuasive ability to prove with logic because you are now attacking the speaker rather than what they are saying. We will discuss the science of anger and negativity in more detail in Chapter 5, but for now, we can identify the persuasion tool as follows: Character attacks are a broken tool and damage your ability to persuade; thus, don't do them. Second, negativity fails because recipients of negativity retreat more to their position, so it is then harder to build bridges to them. In blunt terms, if you are told you are both wrong and stupid, you are less likely to be receptive to discourse than if you are just told you are wrong.

This is where much of the persuasion efforts by some of these op-eds against Senator Helms that we have talked about failed, because they revolved around putting down the character of Senator Helms. Telling him that he is a bigot, or a racist, or not a real Christian because he's not practicing Christianity properly all entail impugning his character. As a tool of persuasion, negativity and character attacks generally always fail because they force the person receiving them to retreat deeper into their position and not engage with you, and not see you as a trustworthy speaker. In this sense, it ties to the importance of credibility, because when you are engaged in negative character attacks on people, you have damaged your credibility to be the person delivering a message that you want to deliver in order to persuade.

Bono could have shown up at Senator Helms's office and charged the senator with being a bigot and a racist and not practicing Christianity properly. This would have failed because Bono would have now forced Senator Helms to defend his own character, and Senator Helms would not have been willing to listen to Bono's discussion about Christianity with an open mind. Bono also would

Let's then take these now-defined persuasion tools to one of our hypotheticals that we all regularly confront, the situation discussed above regarding seeking a pay raise. Take a basic fact pattern that requires persuasion: Last year the company's bonuses were X dollars, and profits were Y dollars, and this year, company profits doubled, and therefore you want a bonus. Let's now employ our persuasion tools and explore how you can best advocate for your raise.

You need credibility, and this requires developing your story, advocacy, and argument to please, prove, and move around a matter on which you have credibility. This requires finding a story from your work for the company of a particular success you had—for example, with a client, a team of employees, or a corporate leadership event. Such an event is something you are an expert on (having done the work) and can authentically discuss to explain your value, meeting both elements of credibility. The right story positively emphasizes your personal connection to the audience and demonstrates that you understand and validate the other side's motivations.

Note immediately where the focus is not: It is not on the company's numbers. If you want to tell C-suite executives and CFO-level people that because the company doubled its profit, it should also double your bonus (or more generally that the company had a great year so you are entitled to more), then you are out of your depth on the financial questions, and immediately they know it. You will not have the expertise or authenticity to carry that argument framed that way. You will be fighting over facts (and logic) that others understand in a richer manner. As a result, you will have defined the terrain on terms that benefit the other side, not you. The response you confront will be in purely financial terms and will revolve around the fact that doubling profit at a corporate level does not translate dollar for dollar the way you think it does. It will be the equivalent from our Bono story of what would have happened if Bono had argued the political merits of what is proper American foreign policy with Senator Helms. That is not to say the company is lying; they may well be speaking the truth about the significance of larger profits, budgeting for larger costs and the like, and you will have engaged on a playing field that does not benefit you.

Thus, you must find a story that you can talk credibly about, and you then can take your core logic and put it to work for your audience. Spend time here to make sure you are aware of whom your audience is when asking for a raise, who exactly decides it, who has the power to grant it. You need to make sure you craft your story to the right audience and speak in the proper way to that audience. Bono did not speak down to Senator Helms. He did not arrive in the senator's office and demand or expect something as if he was owed something; indeed, he went to meet him in his office as opposed to issuing press releases or social media blasts to castigate him. This aspect of respecting your audience, as we saw, was critical, and the same applies to advocating in this hypothetical. You want a raise and believe you earned it, but the same subtle and nuanced difference Bono adopted applies here. You are not simply owed it, and there may be myriad good financial and business-related reasons the company possesses to not grant a bonus. Thus, you need to approach the audience in the same way by respecting the fact that viewpoints can differ while offering a story that justifies your goal.

And be careful with your logic. Arguing that you worked a lot of overtime and so deserve a raise (a form of logic) may be met with the equally logical response that the overtime was already compensated at a high rate so further monies is now even more compensation for already extra-compensated work (or that they will hire more labor and not have you work overtime again). Again, focus your chosen logic on the right story. In this example, it would be explaining, for example, the value and impact of a large project you accomplished that helped the company generate new revenues or perhaps save money, instead of the data and numbers that tell how many hours you spent on a given project.

For example, if your chosen story is the story of a successfully landed client that built important goodwill for your employer to get into potential new markets, which was your achievement, then you can use that to justify the connection between your work and the growth of the company, your value that deserves a raise/reward, and justifies overcoming whatever business reasons may stand against necessarily giving a bonus/raise. This can let you talk about doubled profit/larger bonus logic, but the story that moves that logic along is not just a story of numbers. Your story connects your audience with a personal, valuable event that helped the company, a story that validates the value of the other side's perceptions on bonuses, and this allows you to please, prove, and move your audience to best have the chance to grant you that raise.

Let's go back to Jackie and Diane and assess Jackie's logic. Jackie's logic was as follows: Other firms pay 30 percent more for this position; therefore, I should get 30 percent more. This is a form of inductive reasoning because it takes a specific example (the other firms) and generalizes a conclusion from it (all pay for this position should be the same). The classic example to teach inductive logic is this example: All the swans I have seen are white; therefore, all swans are white. It is true only if indeed the premise holds absolute truth, i.e., the swans I have seen are the same as the entire universe of swans. But what if others have seen black swans? The logic then fails. Jackie's logic hinged on the assumption that all other firms pay 30 percent more and that her few data points actually were correct for all other firms. But it turns out that the data was not absolute. Smaller firms like ours actually paid exactly what she was getting. Her data set did not justify the general conclusion. The logic failed.

Finally, in this exercise, you need to avoid negativity and put-downs. Maybe other employees are not as good as you or have slacked, but you do not need to impugn their character to build yours. Remember, the Cicero rule: Do no harm with your words. Do not put down people, especially those not present to defend themselves, which often makes a listener feel awkward and unsure about your credibility, candor, and honesty. There is always a way to focus on what you did—even when, for example, you may have helped fix someone else's error—without throwing the other person under the bus and looking like you are engaged in negative character attacks. "I showed up as a team player and worked a month without weekends off to get the coding done, and we landed the client with the coding," is better than, "Jane dropped the ball, so I stepped up and worked a month to cover her coding." Both are true. One tells a positive story; the other puts someone down. In short, find a positive story about you and an accomplishment that connects you to the company's success as the vehicle to advocate for your raise, and that puts you in the best position to successfully achieve your persuasion objective, just like Bono did with Senator Helms.

Everyone Can Be a Powerful Persuader

Bono is not a trained professional advocate. It is entirely unclear if he ever conceptualized what he was doing in the specific please, prove, and move persuasion terms that we have discussed here. But he nonetheless engaged in a master class of persuasion as he stood up for his beliefs and positions. Why is this point so important? Because it proves that any one of us, regardless of professional training, can indeed be successful, inspiring, and meaningful persuaders for the issues we may be battling on any given day. Reciprocally, it demonstrates that persuasion is a part of us as humans in our communities and is not an externalized skill set that is the monopoly of some sort of professional class of trained politicians or lawyers.

And if we embrace and are inspired by witnessing, and understanding through stories, the lessons of persuasion, then we

long message on the urgent need to devote resources to winning the Space Race.

> Recognizing the head start obtained by the Soviets with their large rocket engines, which gives them many months of lead time, and recognizing the likelihood that they will exploit this lead for some time to come in still more impressive successes, we nevertheless are required to make new efforts on our own. For while we cannot guarantee that we shall one day be first, we can guarantee that any failure to make this effort will make us last. We take an additional risk by making it in full view of the world, but as shown by the feat of astronaut Shepard, this very risk enhances our stature when we are successful. But this is not merely a race. Space is open to us now; and our eagerness to share its meaning is not governed by the efforts of others. We go into space because whatever mankind must undertake, free men must fully share. I therefore ask the Congress, above and beyond the increases I have earlier requested for space activities, to provide the funds which are needed to meet the following national goals:
>
> First, I believe that this nation should commit itself to achieving the goal, before this decade is out, of landing a man on the moon and returning him safely to the earth. No single space project in this period will be more impressive to mankind, or more important for the long-range exploration of space; and none will be so difficult or expensive to accomplish. We propose to accelerate the development of the appropriate lunar space craft. We propose to develop alternate liquid and solid fuel boosters, much larger than any now being developed, until certain which is superior. We propose additional funds for other engine development and for unmanned explorations—explorations which are particularly important for one purpose which this nation will never overlook: the survival of the man

> who first makes this daring flight. But in a very real sense, it will not be one man going to the moon—if we make this judgment affirmatively, it will be an entire nation. For all of us must work to put him there.[1]

But by 1962, President Kennedy's belief remained highly controversial, and his vision was certainly not one that was a uniformly shared national belief that all Americans had bought into. There was a large chorus of voices that opposed it. Indeed, former President Dwight D. Eisenhower derided the idea as "nuts." Large groups of Republican politicians sought to curtail moon adventures with closer space adventures in Earth's orbit. Even the political left and many leading scientists argued that going to the moon distorted proper priorities and was not possible.[2]

Thus, President Kennedy, to advance his vision, had to speak to the American people in an effort to counter the naysayers and convince the country to walk with him in his chosen uncertain, dangerous, and expensive course of action. Imagine the Herculean task that he confronted in 1962. Indeed, it was only in 1961, a mere year earlier, that the first commercial flight had flown non-stop from Los Angeles to London.[3] Landing on the moon within the decade was the stuff of science fiction and fantasy, a generational leap in technology and advancement over anything ever done or contemplated, an effort that required inventing technology and then executing on the technology, at a staggering cost to the national treasury, all within a few years. Even today in the early twenty-first century, it is a bold, daring claim for a president to lay down the gauntlet and declare that within several years we will walk on the moon again (notably, to this day, none have done it!). For our purposes here, then, it is sufficient to recognize that President Kennedy sought to achieve something genuinely extraordinary, something that confronted staggering odds of failure, and a cause that had legitimate good-faith opposition from scientific, political, and academic quarters.

This brings us to a hot, humid 1962 September day in Houston, Texas, where President Kennedy took the stage at Rice University to speak and make his case to the American people for a moon landing. Known now as the "Moon Speech," President Kennedy's words are a masterclass in one-on-many persuasion. Indeed, from a persuasion perspective on storytelling, metaphors, and moving an audience to your difficult goal, in this author's opinion, it is actually President Kennedy's greatest example of a persuasive speech. Thus, exploring the Moon Speech allows us to identify and double-click on some additional critical aspects of persuasion when we are speaking to groups to advance our cause, be it an executive speaking to his or her corporate team of employees on an issue, you as an employee pitching a new client for your business, or perhaps pitching investors for capital, a mid-level manager speaking to a smaller team on a project, or a parent speaking to a local school board or city council on local issues. All are common one-on-many scenarios that require us to sometimes speak briefly to a larger group who is captive for some short amount of time to our effort to persuade and advocate for an issue.

At the outset, the full speech is incredibly short; the full delivery as spoken was only around eighteen minutes long and 2,000-odd words. The core of the speech for our advocacy exploration is only around 1,000 words reproduced below. This alone is a persuasion lesson we will explore shortly in terms of the profound value of brevity in one's words.

So, let's start by reading the speech, which has been slightly annotated here to allow us to focus on the persuasion lessons it offers us. It is also well worth going to YouTube where you can find and listen to the speech (in full as well as truncated versions) because the nature of his oratorical delivery of the speech has further additional excellent lessons, which we will also discuss at the end of this chapter.[4]

President John F. Kennedy giving his Moon Speech in Houston, Texas, September 12, 1962. Public domain image from the United States government.

But if I were to say, my fellow citizens, that we shall send to the moon, 240,000 miles away from the control station in Houston, a giant rocket more than 300 feet tall, the length of this football field, made of new metal alloys, some of which have not yet been invented, capable of standing heat and stresses several times more than have ever been experienced, fitted together with a precision better than the finest watch, carrying all the equipment needed for propulsion, guidance, control, communications, food and survival, on an untried mission, to an unknown celestial body, and then return it safely to Earth, re-entering the atmosphere at speeds of over 25,000 miles per hour, causing heat about half that of the temperature of the sun—almost as hot as it is here today—and do all this, and do it right, and do it first before this decade is out—then we must be bold.

I'm the one who is doing all the work, so we just want you to stay cool for a minute. [laughter]

However, I think we're going to do it, and I think that we must pay what needs to be paid. I don't think we ought to waste any money, but I think we ought to do the job. And this will be done in the decade of the sixties. It may be done while some of you are still here at school at this college and university. It will be done during the term of office of some of the people who sit here on this platform. But it will be done. And it will be done before the end of this decade.

. . .

Many years ago, the great British explorer George Mallory, who was to die on Mount Everest, was asked why did he want to climb it? He said, "Because it is there."

Well, space is there, and we're going to climb it, and the moon and the planets are there, and new hopes for knowledge and peace are there. And, therefore, as we set sail we ask God's blessing on the most hazardous and dangerous and greatest adventure on which man has ever embarked.[5]

The speech succeeded and galvanized the nation behind the space effort, and before the decade had passed, the United States achieved President Kennedy's goal and landed astronauts on the moon.

Effective Storytelling Can Be Done Using Metaphors to Tell a Story

We talked briefly about Bono's chosen story to take to Senator Helms. But President Kennedy's speech allows us to better explore on a deeper level the primary value of a story to persuasion efforts.

Let's start by exploring what exactly a story is and how using metaphors fits into the larger story structure. First, while we engage with stories all the time in books and movies, it is wrong to think that stories are the province of only brilliant authors or moviemakers and screenwriters. You may not have thought it of yourself (because, you say of yourself, that you are not a creative or a writer), but the truth is that we all are storytellers (yes, you the naysayer, you are too!). At root, stories matter to persuasion because they mediate you as a speaker and the outcome you want. Stories naturally engraft onto human experience in terms of using morality and values in problem solving. Stories are the central bridging mechanism to connect where you are to a desired outcome.

Research has also demonstrated that stories trigger a response in listeners of receptivity at even a bio-chemical level. Paul J. Zak, a PhD neuro-economist and storytelling expert on the neuroscience of narratives, has studied the issue.[6] Dr. Zak and his team studied the effects of moving people via a video story about a boy named Ben with terminal brain cancer and his father, with two video versions of a story shown to participants with subsequent interviews, blood work, and brain MRIs to gauge the empathetic response of the viewers as well as their willingness to donate money to a cancer cause.[7]

The first story had a plot that generated tension and actual character development. "One version shows a father talking to the camera while his two-year-old son, Ben, who has terminal brain cancer, plays in the background. The story has a classic dramatic arc in which the father is struggling to connect to and enjoy his son, all the while knowing that the child has only a few months to live. The clip concludes with the father finding the strength to stay emotionally close to his son 'until he takes his last breath.'"[8]

The second story was also about Ben and his father at the zoo, but intentionally lacked the plot and character development of the first story. This story had a flat narrative. Rather than a story with a plot and character tension addressing the tragic issue of a father confronting his son's terminal cancer diagnosis, "[t]his version does not mention cancer or death, but the boy is bald (from his chemotherapy) and is called 'miracle boy' once during the clip. This video lacks the tension induced by the typical story form but includes the same characters. This version was used as a control story to see what the brain does when any video is being watched."[9]

Participants watched the two videos and were studied, both in terms of their emotional response and also at the chemical, blood level, testing oxytocin levels (that drive empathy) in blood when confronting each story. Participants were given money and an option to donate it to a charity after each separate group viewed the two different videos. Dr. Zak's findings and results were staggering. The first story "with the dramatic arc caused an increase in cortisol and oxytocin. Tellingly, the change in oxytocin had a positive correlation with participants' feeling of empathy for Ben and his father. Heightened empathy motivated participants to offer money to a stranger who was in the experiment. We connected a story to a feeling and then to a prosocial behavior."[10]

In contrast, the second story had a bland narrative of Ben and his father at the zoo. Anyone watching knew it was a story of a boy with brain cancer; the bald head and "miracle boy" reference made that much clear. But there was no plot or drama involved—just the root facts and data about the tragedy—in contrast to the first video that put the facts and data into a story framework of a father trying to cope with his child's imminent death. When they studied the effects on viewers, this second approach "did not increase oxytocin or cortisol, and participants did not report empathy for the story's characters."[11]

Thus, while both short videos demonstrated a tragedy of a terminally ill boy with cancer at the zoo, only one video actually took the facts and data at hand and told a story that was able to connect with the audience and move the audience. The proper story version elicited significantly higher levels of charitable response.[12]

In other words, a properly crafted story induces your audience to be moved and pleased by your persuasion efforts at a chemical level in the brain. As Dr. Zak concludes, there is a universal story structure that connects us as people at a physical and brain level: developed characters confronting tension, trying to resolve a conflict of some kind.[13]

Stories, thus, fundamentally matter to your ability to persuade. At its core, a story has a simple, consistent structure from beginning to middle to end. In the beginning, it has characters (*Jaws*: a shark and people on a boat) that confront an issue that develops a plot and story (the shark has attacked innocents, so the protagonists need to hunt the shark) that leads to a climax (a final battle between man and the shark) that requires at the end a resolution (death of the shark and victory of man over the shark), the resolution sometimes being referred to as the denouement. The story develops through these elements a theme and point of view that the persuader wishes to advance.[14] In other words, in our persuasion context, you start in an initial status quo or steady state (you and your audience), which in turn is disrupted (creating the issue that needs your persuasion efforts), and this then requires the unfolding of a story to transform, or move, the original steady state to a new one (the climax and outcome of your success in persuasion that achieves your goal). This is why a story visually depicts in a graph as an arced line of building tension from the flat initial state to the climax and then to a falling state of resolution, in distinction to a flat line (flat narrative).

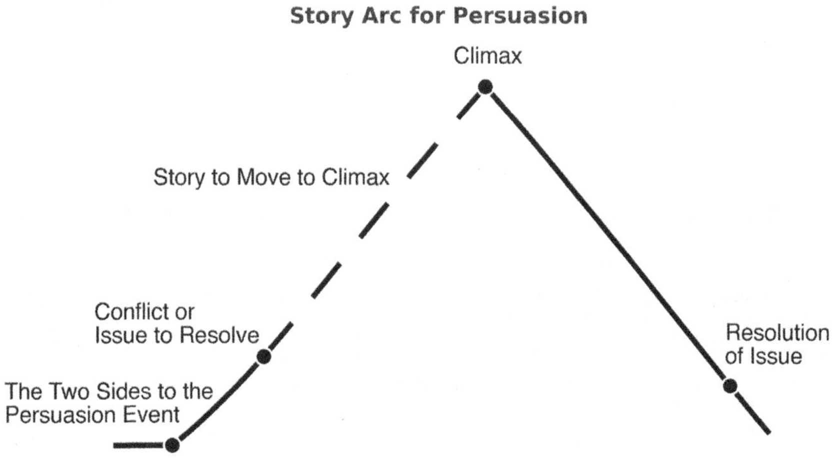

The Story Arc graph in persuasion terms.

Metaphors are a part of storytelling. Metaphors are a tool we use to compare two things—one more abstract, the other more concrete—in order to move an audience in persuasion. A basic example of one is, "My love for you is an eternal rose." This allows connections to be created between abstract ideas and more relatable and concrete human experiences. (I can tell my wife I love her repeatedly but expressing love with a metaphor like the one above gives it deeper, richer meaning as it connects the abstract "love" to a tangible, beautiful rose.) And for persuasion purposes, as stated by the National Storytelling Network, "Such metaphoric byways and pathways enable us to explore the ideas, forces, and powers that lie behind or beyond our rational thought."[15] Often, absent a metaphor in storytelling, we do not have a powerful vehicle to deliver the core persuasion we are trying to achieve to touch the emotion of the listener. But when we touch emotion, we move people to our viewpoint as opposed to living only in the logical work of proving with rationality. (Similes, the cousin of metaphors, are another tool of persuasion that are similar but less abstract than metaphors. Similes compare one thing to another often using the word "like" to draw the connection, i.e., "Your heart is like a bloomed rose.")

Now let's unpackage stories and metaphors as used by President Kennedy to persuade his audience, echoing the Steve Jobs quote at the outset on the primacy of stories, to his values and agenda. Recall, in 1962, the average person in his or her late fifties or sixties had been born into a world without commercial aircraft and that had only telegraph and radio, and already in that lifespan had seen technology leap forward with television, early computers, ubiquitous phones, nuclear power, orbiting satellites, and commercial air travel connecting continents, to name a few. President Kennedy confronted an overwhelming task: convincing the reticent public and naysayers that additional investments had to be made in further new, unimaginable technologies, all in an age where society had already experienced massive technological change with all the attendant ills, or confusion, that rapid change brings upon society.

President Kennedy crafted a story to address this tension. His central story was humankind's history of achievement, the history of humanity's development and ability to overcome impossible situations as a means of mastering and controlling our world and harnessing it for our betterment. Recall that his speech traced humankind's history, from discovering fire to early physics concepts to the steam engine to nuclear power.

To build this story, President Kennedy settled on a metaphor to compare the abstract issue of human and technological development over tens of thousands of years—an abstract and hard-to-conceptualize issue—into a fifty-year time period. Everyone can comprehend a fifty-year time window given it is within the average lifespan. And this adds a sense of urgency and pace to the story. If 50,000 years is seen as a fifty-year window, then humans first created shelter five years ago, two months ago humans created steam power, and last week penicillin was discovered, all with gradations in between, but this metaphorical timeclock construct demonstrates massive recent development and contextualizes the long history of advancement in a tangible manner.

This enabled President Kennedy to counter an opposition narrative (to persuade against his opponents) and show that human achievement was long and slow over time, but suddenly now breathtaking and amazing, and that our society in that precise moment possessed a unique moment of potential, part of the entire fabric of history's march of progress. And critically, he used the timeclock metaphor to show that many great achievements were uniquely a product of western ingenuity and borne from an unwillingness to recoil in the face of challenge, the core of the American experiment. This brilliant timeclock metaphor allowed him to deliver a story of achievement and progress—where humankind was a central character, and America was the current protagonist character—that pushed the listener to answer the pregnant climactic question: Do we remain a part of that amazing, rapid history of development, or do we regress? No one chooses regression in the face of that story; instead they choose—as the answer and denouement to the climactic question that President Kennedy's story led us toward—the optimism of continuing the successful journey. President Kennedy's chosen story was exactly the type of story that Dr. Zak discerned creates emotional and physical reactions in the listener that enable the speaker's ability to persuade.

What if President Kennedy had just made the facts and data pitch without that timeclock metaphor? That is, what if President Kennedy delivered a flat narrative story as in Dr. Zak's second story?

President Kennedy could have simply detailed American and historical achievements and argued that this was the next chapter in the story—after all, that was the root issue anyway. But that would have lacked the powerful story that the metaphor of the timeclock allowed him to build—it would have lacked the plot of humankind's urgent, rapid development of technology to achieve, and it would have lacked the existence of humanity as the central character and America as the character picking up the baton of history. Likewise, it would not have possessed the dramatic plot of human history that moved slow at first, but now in very recent times moves fast, where all great aspects of human history are directly connected to one another, rendering this next moment (the climax, do we embrace the moon challenge?) simply the next piece of the chain of history. Absent the story's metaphor connecting the Space Race to all of human history's positive development and the necessary imperative that America continue on as the current inheritor of all of humankind's history of achievement, the persuasion effort would not be as powerful as it would not be a story that compelled the listener to answer the climatic question and agree that resources today should go to space rather than other pressing social issues.

President Kennedy's metaphorical story followed the arc of a basic story as we discussed above. He identified a point of contention (should we try to go the moon?), developed a plot and explored the characters in it (Americans, Soviets, and which group is inheriting the legacy of humankind's history of achievement), and built the story to a climactic point of tension (all of history's rapid and amazing breakthroughs inexorably lead to this next chapter in space), where the resolution, or denouement, was then obvious to the listener (we want to be the inheritors of that great legacy and do the impossible again, like our forebearers). By developing the persuasion activity through this metaphor-laden story of a timeclock, he established a story structure that impelled—indeed, compelled—the listener to agree that Americans had to go to space even though it was extremely uncertain and difficult. This story allowed him to move his audience to his persuasive vision, far more than offering logical arguments about the political value of beating the Soviets to compel the audience to agree.

Indeed, the brilliance of the metaphorical story employed is that the very reasons not to go—potential death, grave uncertainty, extreme expense—actually became the reasons we had to go. "We choose to go to the moon. We choose to go to the moon in this decade and do the other things, not because they are easy, but because they are hard ...." President Kennedy moved the audience because he made the arguments of its impossibility the actual arguments of its possibility, by persuading that it is the impossible (the "hard") that America has always done.

Nowhere is this ability to use a story and a meaningful phrase more powerful than when one considers these words: "Many years ago, the great British explorer George Mallory, who was to die on Mount Everest, was asked why did he want to climb it? He said, 'Because it is there.' Well, space is there, and we're going to climb it ...." Having persuaded Americans that choosing to go was the right choice, because the spirit of adventure and doing the impossible is what America does, he managed to take an example of someone who died doing the near impossible and turn it into a reason we had to go. After all, Mallory died trying to summit Mount Everest! If someone asked you to go white water rafting, but said that people die quite regularly on the rapids, you would never go. But here President Kennedy turned the issue on its head with the power of his story and metaphor.

Finally, imagine a different story as follows: President Kennedy could have declared that his scientists were right and other scientists were wrong, that he was not "nuts" and that it was President Eisenhower who was in fact "nuts." How would this approach have played out? First, his ability to please would have been damaged, because he would have been staking a side in a divided scientific-academic dispute where there was genuine uncertainty. That is, he would have suddenly lacked humility and staked his credibility on one side, demanding the other was just wrong. His genius in avoiding this debate, indeed by embracing the uncertainty, allowed him to recognize and respect that the audience could differ on the underlying scientific questions, but still take his side nonetheless. Second, this also allowed him to avoid a story whose logic could falter under the weight of arguments about which scientists were really correct on the issue, a problem that would have damaged his ability to prove and would have further damaged the success of his endeavor if there were future misfortunes (as in fact unfolded when Apollo 1's astronauts all died in their capsule).

Let's pivot here to a real-world application for you when speaking to a group; take as an example a project on which you have a team to lead on their need to finish the project within a deadline. Your superiors and corporate executives have said they need this project done by a certain time. You have to perform and must get your team to do their respective jobs to finish the project. How do you meet with your team to motivate them—to persuade them—that they need to give their all to the project?

One approach is to make clear that upper-level management has demanded this, their jobs are on the line, and they must get to work without fail and perform. This is the standard "persuasive" pitch given in these circumstances, treating the project as a job necessity and thus no more need be said. It's another way of saying that your job is to do this, it is demanded of you, the company wants this project so they can make more money, you must do it—and all of that is decidedly true, of course. But does that actually give the team a larger story of why their work matters? It does not, and here is where a simple story can be developed to make your team a part of a larger story, themselves important actors in the drama.

and move an audience if employed well. A catchy theme articulated in a few words that captures your goal and is repeated a few times, or even a mere word choice that is repeated a few times, creates symmetry to a presentation and leaves a lasting impression about the topic. The act of repeating a particular sound—the words themselves—adds a lyrical element to the speech and captures attention and creates a formed impression in the mind of the listener. The most famous example, perhaps, is Martin Luther King Jr.'s, "I have a dream." The phrase was used only eight times in his near-eighteen-minute speech, but it built a foundation for his persuasive argument and was so successful that most people know the phrase, even when they do not know or remember the entire speech.

President Kennedy's one-on-many persuasion effort employed positive word rhythms in his speech in different ways, and the Moon Speech gives us two clear examples of how to move an audience with word rhythms that move an audience. We will look at both examples, because one is of the "I have a dream" kind, but the other, equally important one was also used to build a foundation for his persuasion effort to anchor his words and move the audience.

Trademark-like Word Rhythms

The first example: "<u>Why choose</u> this as our goal? And they may well ask <u>why</u> climb the highest mountain? <u>Why</u>, 35 years ago, fly the Atlantic? <u>Why</u> does Rice play Texas? <u>We choose to go</u> to the moon. <u>We choose to go</u> to the moon in this decade and do the other things, not because they are easy, but because they are hard ...." President Kennedy repeated this "choose" phrase only two times and presaged it with the word "choose" two sentences before, for three uses of the "why choose" concept. Those mere four words—we choose to go—are a powerful message of self-affirmation and choice, of strength and not passivity, of inclusive self-determination to face obstacles, and the four words telegraph that we are not afraid of failure. While the four-word phrase was used only twice, the words have become a shorthand symbol of the speech and persuasion afoot, functioning almost like a trademark of sorts. Listeners understood "we choose to go" to have monumental emotional and logical meaning as a battle cry (that is, they were moved and hence persuaded!) to signify a dedication to achieve the impossible and willingly fight overwhelming odds. Indeed, you can buy hats and pins with "We choose to go" printed on them precisely because the words convey the story and theme so powerfully. The phrase worked because it was the right shorthand encapsulation of his story and because it was planted a few times in repetitive fashion to anchor the idea in the listener's mind; each time he utters it, as with Martin Luther King Jr.'s uttering "I have a dream," the flag that was placed in the ground by the phrase's first use is further hammered in.

Related, President Kennedy, as we see, also framed four "why" questions to trigger the "choose" phrase. By asking the "why" questions, he invoked the naysayers' concerns—his antagonists in the story. But he then dispatched with the counter concerns by answering them with his "choose" concept, explaining, humorously, that Rice plays Texas in college football for the same reason we crossed the Atlantic: because it is a challenge we willingly embrace and we must confront because the act of trying is the relevant journey itself.

Word Vibrations from Word and Structure Repetition

The second example of positive word rhythms is seen in a few passages. The first: "Despite the striking fact that most of the scientists that the world has ever known are alive and working today, despite the fact that this nation's own scientific manpower is doubling every 12 years in a rate of growth more than three times that of our population as a whole, despite that, the vast stretches of the unknown and the unanswered and the unfinished still far outstrip our collective comprehension." This method of oral or written persuasion works because the repeat word "despite" and alliteration from the words beginning with "un"—even if it is not memorable trademark-like slogans as we already addressed—anchors the words and content in the listener's mind. It is like a catchy musical lyric that you inevitably remember or a short burst of musical notes that repeats and is memorable.

Another example of finding positive word vibrations for your persuasion to please your audience's ear and move them is seen in this opening construct, almost the very first words out of the president's mouth: "We meet in an hour of change and challenge, in a decade of hope and fear, in an age of both knowledge and ignorance." President Kennedy three times uses the "in an/a" construct followed by two contrasting words: change and challenge/hope and fear/knowledge and ignorance. That structure of three concepts (hour, decade, age) each with two alternating aspects to them leaves a memorable imprint on a listener's mind as it creates a rhythmic structure that conveys ideas.

Finally, note the repeat usage of the "why" and "choose" word rhythms, and the other repeating word structures we discussed, were used only a few times, just enough to catch the listeners' attention, but it was not overbearing. If the phrase is repeated too much (no more than three times is a good rule of thumb), it loses its power, and this brings us to brevity in another respect.

The Value of Brevity to Persuasion Efforts

Brevity is itself a key aspect of successful persuasion. All too often, people believe that quantity matters and so they talk too much in their efforts to persuade. Monopolizing time and space with words, however, is not a substitute or even an adjunct to successful persuasion. Brevity is important because a message is best heard and received when it is delivered with concise clarity in an efficient manner. Brevity demonstrates confidence; undue wordiness demonstrates a lack of conviction. At the same time, brevity is important because an audience has limited bandwidth to be persuaded, and if one drones on for too long, the audience starts wandering. Finally, brevity shows that you respect your audience and the value of its time, which enables you to secure an audience's buy-in to listen to you.

Here, President Kennedy's speech on such a momentous issue of national significance was a mere seventeen and a half minutes in delivery, essentially a quarter of an hour. It was not the hours and hours of speeches we see from our elected officials or the hours of political debates, nor even the multi-hour-long form podcast discussions that are popular these days to try to make their points. If he had spent an hour making his case, the audience would have lost patience and wandered, no longer listening even as their minds moved.

But for a quarter of an hour, people can and will reciprocate and give you their focus and attention. This is the lesson of persuasion: President Kennedy demonstrated his respect for the audience by not forcing them to listen to him for too long, and so they could reciprocate by giving him the attention he sought. Respect your audience back by respecting their time—let them know at the outset that you will speak for only two or five minutes or whatever your small allotment is—and then you have buy-in from the audience to truly listen as you make your persuasion points concisely. And President Kennedy spoke at an ideal pace for public speaking and presentations, which is about 120 words per minute, so do not try to be brief on time by speaking so rapidly that nobody can internalize your words!

to engage in that aggressive back-and-forth. If Mary had tried to rise to that occasion by being like Jack, she would have been performing as someone she was not, she would have been fake to her personality, and after even a few minutes of that, the audience of judges would have broken her.

After a couple of minutes, the judges noticeably looked disarmed as their level of hostility did not match her tone, and it probably appeared to them that they were being overbearing. (We will discuss this in more detail later as it relates to the critical idea of reciprocity in persuasion.) The result was that the judges actually sat back in their big black leather chairs high up on the courtroom bench, and one of them even put his hands together with his fingers under his jaw as he listened to her. As Mary spoke at the podium, the powerful federal judges just listened to her, and even the opposing government lawyer turned to watch her. All eyes and ears were on her as she engaged in confident persuasive advocacy. She was the epitome of an authentic speaker, being herself. Her comfort at being herself and not trying to perform in the manner that some may feel they need to do to meet the moment—to perform as Jack or to perform like the judges—was exactly what allowed her to gain the respect of the judges who actually listened to her.

Mary performed a master class at public persuasive speaking, even though she had what she perceived were personality traits that limited her own perception of her ability to be a powerful speaker. Her authenticity as a speaker, an improved version of herself from where she started the academic year (practice, practice, practice—it works!), disarmed the hostility of the judges and actually forced them to listen to what she had to say and respect her message. Mary spoke calmly and with a hint of shyness, but firmly. Although she did not speak with the comfort, soft humor, and soaring language of John F. Kennedy as he delivered his Moon Speech, nor the natural pace and aggression of Jack, she delivered as masterful a presentation for her issue as the president did for his. Because Mary performed the best version of herself without trying to fake a different personality—her effort at improving herself as opposed to changing herself—her authenticity captured the judges' attention, and they were receptive and willing to listen to her and potentially be persuaded by her.

This is the core lesson that comes from efforts at public persuasive speaking as it relates to being authentic: Regardless of what you perceive your limits to be or your comparative perceptions of better speakers, disregard those perceptions and simply work to make yourself the best version of yourself. *That* will command the respect of your audience and give you the best chance at being persuasive, because you will have established your authenticity and, therefore, your ability to move and please your audience. Put differently, improve your lane; do not try to change lanes.

Persuasion Tools Distilled from President Kennedy's Moon Speech Story

In this chapter, we developed the foundational building blocks of a story: There is a point of contention or issue to confront (the struggle the story will address) between characters (you and the person you are persuading, for example) that sets up, in turn, the use of the story that is developed to lead to the ultimate issue being addressed (the climax), where that climactic resolution of the issue is resolved in your favor as the natural consequence of the chosen story/metaphors employed by you (denouement). We identified the questions you need to ask yourself to help pinpoint your proper story.

We also studied the use of metaphors to develop a persuasive story, because metaphors can make complicated concepts easier to access for the listener you are trying to prove your point to and then move by way of persuasion.

As a means of pleasing the audience and moving the audience to your viewpoint, we looked at the use, sparingly but sufficiently, of word rhythms, both trademark/logo-like phrases and repeat words and word structures as memorable anchors to ideas. A good rule of thumb is to repeat a rhythmic idea or structure three times.

We also looked at brevity as part of your credibility in terms of pleasing the audience in persuasion, while recognizing that you cannot speak so rapidly that you lose your audience either.

Finally, we stressed the importance of establishing credibility to please the listener by way of being your best version of yourself and not faking a character or trying to perform to some motif or archetype that you are not but that you wrongly think is needed to be effective; be yourself and focus on improving and hewing to your innate default personality, not engaging in personality changes that are not you.

Thus far, we have seen stories of persuasion around the issue of AIDS relief and the Space Race, but now let's turn to an issue that is profoundly emotional and hurtful to many, more personal, perhaps, than the Space Race or foreign AIDS relief: the issue of flag burning and whether one should have the right to so hurt and offend others by their speech. In the twenty-first century, the issue of hate speech is as powerful as ever, with society as divided as ever over whether one can engage in hate speech freely or whether the speech can be limited because it offends and hurts innocents. Let's now delve into this polarizing area where beliefs are very powerfully held on each side for very root philosophical reasons—a common divide we all find ourselves in across myriad social, political, economic, business, or personal areas of life—and let's see persuasion at work in this difficult forum of hotly debated, divisive social issues.

Key Takeaways

- Stories follow a familiar arc: characters who confront an issue that develops a plot that leads to a climax that requires at the end a resolution of the conflict in a manner compelled by the story that built the plot. Metaphors are powerful elements to use to tell a story.
- Stories are the central bridging mechanism to connect where you are to a desired outcome. And stories, in comparison to flat narratives (facts and data), trigger physiological reactions in the listener, prompting empathy and receptivity to the story.
- Carefully chosen words or phrases repeated a few times, often with alliteration, allow you to move an audience with your story and create a memorable takeaway (if in doubt, three is a good number to hew to in terms of the repetition).
- Brevity shows respect to your audience and builds reciprocally the audience's willingness to give you their attention.
- Regardless of what you perceive your limits to be or your comparative perceptions of better speakers, disregard those perceptions and create the best version of yourself to maintain authenticity and please (improve your lane; don't change lanes).

But then the protesters proceeded to Dallas City Hall where they gathered in a circle, took out an American flag, and lit it on fire. Some spat on the flag while it burned; others chanted anti-American sentiments. No one was injured, and various local residents stopped to watch this event unfold. Shortly after the flag burning, Dallas police arrived and arrested around a hundred protesters, mostly for disorderly conduct.[2]

However, Gregory Lee Johnson was one protester arrested for flag desecration. Johnson later described the 1984 Republican Convention in Dallas as delivering a "theme of toxic American chauvinism" with loads of American flags lining the streets. "And then we burned the American flag in front of the convention center. That was a real juxtaposition of red, white, and blue chauvinism and in defiance against that, our standing with the people of the world."[3]

Under Texas state law at that time, the act of intentionally desecrating the national flag where the flag burner knows it will seriously offend someone was a crime. Johnson refused to plea and went to trial arguing that he had a First Amendment right to burn the flag to convey his message and ideas. The Dallas assistant district attorney argued that the flag burning was not speech and instead was conduct outside the First Amendment, and even if it was speech, it was no different from other speech that can be restricted such as lewd commentary or yelling "fire" in a theatre. The jury convicted Johnson of illegal flag burning and sentenced him to a year in jail and a $2,000 fine without probation.[4] He appealed, and his case eventually reached the United States Supreme Court for argument in 1989.

The question posed by his arrest and conviction is whether the act of flag burning is protected speech within the First Amendment or whether it is not protected speech and is outside the First Amendment. It is a political and social issue that is divisive in society, of course. Most people find abhorrent the act of burning a flag, the uniform symbol of the United States.[5] Soldiers go to war for the United States wearing the flag on their uniforms, so as a symbol, it has immense meaning to millions of Americans. And very few people ever burn a flag precisely because it is such a serious act. But at the same time, many believe that the act of flag burning is powerful speech to convey messages and ideas and should be permitted to deliver one's viewpoint without the restriction of state criminal laws denying the right. One can ponder each side of this debate and see pros and cons of each side: Is it speech, or is it really conduct? If conduct, can it be regulated? If speech, how can it be limited when other speech is free? Do we allow government regulation of speech that is harmful or offensive to viewers? Fraudulent speech can be regulated by fraud laws, and false advertising speech can be regulated by consumer protection laws, so why can't the government also regulate flag burning? Or, reciprocally, do we actually value and demand that the First Amendment requires us to be exposed to certain harmful and offensive speech? Pondering each side of these questions, we can recognize that reasonable people of good faith may come to different conclusions about where these social and legal lines are drawn.

And this makes framing the exact persuasion argument you want to adopt so critical, because when people can divide over a such an issue—as many issues we constantly discuss and debate in our persuasive efforts are so divisive—what exactly you decide to settle on for your story and argument can make all the difference in your ability to persuade your audience.

When this issue of flag burning made its way to the United States Supreme Court, an attorney named William Kunstler argued for flag burning to be protected. Kunstler had been a long-time, famed, if not infamous, civil rights lawyer, and in the 1960s, had represented the Chicago Seven in the highly publicized trial where the government alleged that the defendants engaged in violence and a conspiracy to incite a riot at the 1968 Democratic National Convention in Chicago.[6] During the period of that trial, Kunstler danced and demonstrated outside with his clients, and found himself in such bitter arguments in court with the trial judge—a judge who shockingly bound and gagged one of the defendants in front of the jury—that Kunstler was sentenced by the trial judge to four years in prison for contempt of court. A higher court later reversed the prison sentence.[7]

On the other side, Dallas Assistant District Attorney General Kathi Alyce Drew appeared for the State of Texas to argue that flag burning was subject to state criminal regulation and outside the First Amendment. This was Drew's first appearance in the Supreme Court on behalf of Texas.

Supreme Court watchers and constitutional law and civil rights experts expected Texas to win the case given the case's backdrop and the conservative makeup of the Supreme Court.[8] This brings us to the oral arguments, two in total, to allow us to explore some critical persuasion lessons from the two advocates, Kunstler and Drew.

Attorney William Kunstler (left) and his client Gregory Lee Johnson (right). By Joel Seidenstein, Creative Commons Attribution—Share Alike 3.0, creativecommons.org/licenses/by-sa/3.0/deed.en.

Overreaching Arguments Damage Your Ability to Persuade. To Avoid This, Genuinely Ponder Your Logic and Argument by Actively Spending Time Inhabiting the Other Side's Point of View.

Drew for the State of Texas began. She immediately stood up and told the Supreme Court that she would concede flag burning is symbolic speech and would instead argue that even as speech, it could be regulated by government, because government interests in banning that speech overrode the individual's interests in the speech.

We can pause here to unpackage the argument she settled on as it had dire consequences for the outcome of the case. By agreeing that flag burning was speech within the First Amendment, she now had to justify treating it as a form of disfavored speech that could nonetheless be regulated. The argument that the flag burning act is symbolic speech you can see triggers all sorts of difficult line-drawing questions for the listener immediately: If the government can control this speech because it offends or hurts, can it punish someone for calling someone a vulgar name? Can it punish someone for expressing an anti-Europe sentiment that offends the Irish-American community? The list goes on, and you get the point.

"We believe that preservation of the flag as a symbol of nationhood and national unity is a compelling and valid state interest. We feel very certain that Congress has the power to both adopt a national symbol and to take steps to prevent the destruction of that symbol, to protect the symbol," Drew argued.[9]

Having chosen that argument, the Supreme Court justices almost exploded. The first justice to pounce on her was the conservative Justice Antonin Scalia.

"Now, why does … why does the … why did the defendant's actions here destroy the symbol? His actions would have been useless unless the flag was a very good symbol for what he intended to show contempt for. His action does not make it any less a symbol."[10]

to argue it was conduct that can be regulated, or that even as speech, it was subject to regulation because there need to be narrow, appropriate limits to our ability to offend or hurt with speech in public. But having chosen to abandon those arguments, Texas was stuck arguing that it can regulate human respect for certain symbols. This exact set of concerns about the logic of your persuasion effort animates all your persuasive efforts even when you are discussing things far less lofty than flag burning at the Supreme Court.

Let's go back to an example we have used before about dangerous logic that has no boundaries: The company made $X last year, and bonuses were $Y. This year it made $2X, so bonuses should be $2Y. That is a standard version of logic that has surface appeal—the same way burning a flag is so horrible it should be outlawed, but the moment you pause and consider the ramifications, you realize it is full of holes. What if the company has to invest heavily in a new business area and needs capital for that? What if its profits were the result of tax issues that do not translate to actual cash? What if a recession may be looming, or new competition, and the company has concerns about the next six or twelve months and its survival. All of those serious issues are simply ignored by the rush to employ surface-level logic.

To proceed with logic, it must be logic that is sound and can persuade the listener when wrapped in a story. To find the logic to your story for your persuasive effort, you have to think about the meaning of what you are saying and ask yourself how that may not make sense. How exactly do we do this? Put yourself in the shoes of the recipient and spend real time thinking of all the things that may run against your logic; make a genuine effort to see the other side and contemplate all that may be wrong with your argument. All too often, we do not do this because we want to see only the argument we have latched onto and do not want to embrace the other side. But to have the best chance of persuading, you have to actually inhabit the mind of the other side by doing this exercise. That will then inform you of the propriety or not of your logic and help you find the right logic to develop the right persuasive pitch. When you have a list, see how your logic fares against that list. If your logic does not address those holes, then your logic—and the story you were building with it (profits doubled, so it is only fair that bonuses double, in our example)—is denying you the ability to compose a compelling story to persuade the listener.

For Texas, in the flag burning case, it failed to inhabit the other side and recognize that its story and argument permitted forced compulsion of respect to books, flowers, or other symbols; it failed to see the overreach in its logic.

One of the cardinal lessons I teach in my persuasion classes with my students is exactly this point of inhabiting the other side's mind. We have federal appeals we prepare for oral argument, and we spend months refining our argument to persuade. Midway through preparing our appeal, I require the students to stop everything and now become our adversary. They must spend a week making the best arguments against us that they can muster. It is difficult, and students find it painful at times, because it challenges the logic and story they have being creating and are wed to. But it pays immense dividends. After a week of doing this and then actively presenting the other side's argument, every single time we find gaps in our own logic and argument that we can then learn from to refine our persuasion effort. This is exactly how you are not stuck, as John Stuart Mill's chapter outset quote laments, knowing only your side of the issue; this is how you know the other side's best arguments so that you may then work to persuade against them.

This brings us back to our two real-world characters from the Introduction, Jackie and Diane. Recall, Jackie wanted the large raise and had compiled data to show what other firms paid their employees with similar titles. She showed the specific instance and reasoned that the salary from that specific instance should apply to her (a form of inductive reasoning as we discussed in Chapter 1). Part of what damaged Jackie's effort at persuasion was that the logic of the data was subject to question—her inductive reasoning was wrong. Yes, those jobs paid that much more. But when we really looked at the data, those other law firms were much larger with far higher revenues than our small firm; those employees were in large metropolitan cities, not the suburbs like us; they were in-office, whereas we allow all of our employees to work remote all the time; and smaller firms like ours paid what she was already receiving. The specific circumstances did not generate a general principle that was equal for us. And so, if Jackie had spent time inhabiting our viewpoint and challenged herself to figure out what was wrong with her logic, then she would have realized that her chosen effort at proving would not work. Inhabiting the other side is critical to unmask errors in logic and, in turn, illuminate the right persuasive story to pick. Perhaps if she had inhabited our world more carefully, she would have then developed a better persuasive story, like Diane did.

Inhabiting the other side's position is critical to persuasion, thus, for two distinct but related reasons. First, and simply, it allows you to find the flaws in your stated position. Second, and critically, it regularly reveals that you do not have a monopoly on truth in an issue and that reasonable minds can disagree on vast amounts of topics. This second point is critical because it stops you from drinking the proverbial Kool-Aid and, in turn, allows you to recalibrate your argument to one that remains persuasive but also demonstrates respect—not disrespect—for the other side. For when you disrespect the other side, you quickly lose the ability to find common ground that is necessary to persuade by pleasing your audience.

The Flag Burning Supreme Court Arguments Continue

After Drew presented her argument, Kunstler had his time to make his argument. Rather than a broad argument that risked losing Justice Scalia, Kunstler took a decidedly narrow argument. Speech like flag burning can be limited sometimes, he asserted, but only if it poses a clear and present danger to the community (such as the oft-cited example of being allowed to delimit one from yelling "fire" in a movie theatre). Here, Kunstler explained, "If you're going to stop it, it has to be so imminent … it has to be so imminent that it really reaches clear and present danger proportions. … I think that is the rule here. … I think you must at least show some clear and present danger, some imminence. … I would just like to end my argument—I think this is a fundamental First Amendment case, that the First Amendment to the written Constitution is in jeopardy by statutes like this. … 'Those who begin coercive elimination of dissent soon find themselves eliminating dissenters.'"[19]

That is a narrow argument (and story) because he did not argue the state can never regulate flag burning (he did not argue the opposite of Drew, namely that flag burning was sacrosanct); instead, he argued that the state can ban flag burning but it must meet a higher test of potentially causing danger to the community (in distinction to the counter argument that it can be regulated because it offends). And, as you may remember from the earlier discussion above, the flag burning in Dallas that August 1984 day was decidedly peaceful. Kunstler, in turn, grounded that narrow argument, which permitted the importance of respect for the flag, in a story of protection of dissenting views, which, if not done, will soon find all of us "dissenters" subject to being eliminated.

Compare Kunstler's story to Drew's. Kunstler offered a story built on the idea that eliminating dissent starts us down a road that eliminates all dissent, which means any one of us, depending upon

But the Case Continues: Own Your Errors and Mistakes to Build Your Credibility

Despite winning the case, a year later, a second Supreme Court oral argument in the flag burning cases occurred.[23] This quirk of fate occurred on the same issue of the constitutionality of flag burning under the First Amendment, because in the interim, Congress, due to public disapproval of the Supreme Court's ruling, had passed a federal law banning flag burning.[24] That now required the Supreme Court to address the federal law and whether it met the First Amendment, instead of the Texas state criminal law that it had addressed in the *Texas v. Johnson* case. And this second oral argument allows us to explore one other very critical tool of persuasion as it relates to having the character to own your mistakes—to build your credibility—instead of trying to obfuscate your errors, instead of denying, instead of ducking and weaving to avoid responsibility.

To explore this, we need to return to something Kunstler said to Justice Stevens in the *Texas v. Johnson* case we discussed.

In that original argument, Justice Stevens asked, "Do you think the federal government has any power at all to … to regulate how this flag is displayed in public places?"[25]

Kunstler: "I don't believe so …."

Justice Stevens was surprised, "There's no state interest whatsoever?"

Kunstler doubled down, "I don't see any state interest whatsoever."[26]

Justice Stevens, a World War II veteran, was, by accounts, aghast at the answer. Law clerks later said Justice Stevens was "infuriated," and others in court that day saw Justice Stevens turn visibly red and angry.[27]

Let's pause; why was Justice Stevens so angry? Kunstler had overstated the issue—he had argued too aggressively, and, although his point was secondary to the core analysis and argument he was pushing, he was not correct in fact. The federal government certainly can demand that flags be displayed in public parks in a particular way (i.e., not upside down), and Kunstler just overstated the argument in his probable attempt to take the position that the flag should be off-limits from government regulation. In the moment of that exchange, he made an overbroad argument and made a mistake and, in the process, offended a veteran who obviously wanted to know government flags could have some level of respect on public property. Kunstler could have conceded that the government can regulate the display of a government flag on public property while at the same time saying Johnson had the right to burn his flag; the two are not inconsistent at all, and had Kunstler hewed to that argument, he would have taken the narrower path we discussed above. Ultimately, Kunstler's position in response to Justice Stevens's question was wrong within the law and overstated his case. He erred. Now, he still won the case (although Justice Stevens voted against him), and so that error did not cause him to lose the case, but it was a mistake he made in the heat of the moment. Ultimately, he survived the misstep, because of the narrow 5-4 decision and because it was not a central point on which the entire argument hinged.

United States Supreme Court, 1988-90. Justice Scalia is standing on the far left, and Justice Stevens is standing next to Justice Scalia. Public domain image from the United States government.

But a year later, Kunstler was back at the Supreme Court again to challenge Congress's attempt to ban flag burning. He remembered that exchange from the year before. In the second outing on flag burning before the United States Supreme Court, the case was called and Kunstler went to the podium to talk to the justices and explain his argument. And in the very first few sentences he uttered, he immediately took responsibility for his error.

"Now, the Court ... I must say to the Court, in rereading what I said last time in the *Texas v. Johnson* case, I want a little mea culpa. In responding to Justice Stevens, I believe, I said that the government had no legitimate interest in enacting any legislation about the flag. I think I was wrong in that respect, and this Court, of course, did not adopt that argument, and I think rightly so. I am persuaded that there are things the government can do with reference to the flag. They can do many things to persuade people to respect it, to fly it, to indicate how it should be flown, to indicate the dimensions, to indicate the type of flag it should be and how it should appear, and they do that in part under Title 36 U.S.C. 173 to 177, but they cannot do it in a penal way. So I express my mea culpa here in response to that question a year ago that Justice Stevens asked of me."[28]

This is perhaps the most significant lesson from the flag burning persuasion exercise that we can distill, and it is one most overlooked by people in their day-to-day persuasion activities. If we misstate something or make a mistake, rather than double down and obfuscate it or avoid owning it, take it head-on as Kunstler did and own it. By accepting responsibility voluntarily without demand, you immediately tell the person you are trying to persuade that you have the character to admit fault and own it. And remember, the very first aspect we discussed in all our profiles here is the importance of credibility with your audience. People are willing to accept that you make mistakes; what damages your credibility is trying to avoid it or escape it by cute language designed to deny or deflect. *Those* acts damage credibility.

There is a secondary critical aspect to the value of owning mistakes. By conceding your error, you deflate the other side's potential line of attack against your words, and you push them to have to accept your apology. That requires them to be aboveboard in dealing with you. And if they refuse, then they lose their credibility—who in good faith cannot accept an apology, after all? If they refuse, then it shows their credibility is weakened in the discussion.

At bottom, we all make mistakes sometimes. And we often fail to accept responsibility for them, instead finding ways to justify our error. That model of persuasion ultimately damages your effectiveness in pleasing your audience and hence damages your credibility as a persuader. To err is human. To own errors is to persuade, because you show sincerity and authenticity.

CHAPTER 4

The Bishop Takes on the Roman Empire

"Danger lies in the writer becoming the victim of his own exaggeration, losing the exact notion of sincerity, and in the end coming to despise the truth itself as something too cold, too blunt for his purpose …."

—Joseph Conrad, *A Personal Record*, 1912

The Ancient Roman Senate's Pagan Altar of Victory: Save It or Abandon It?

For hundreds of years, the ancient Roman Senate had an Altar of Victory with a statue of the goddess of victory, Victoria. This particular statue was placed on the altar in 29 BCE by Augustus after a military victory, and the statue was apparently the work of a Greek artist. The statue was a solid gold rendition of Victoria, who was personified as a winged woman in a long and flowing robe standing on a circular orb and holding a palm leaf or laurel wreath.

At this Altar of Victory, senators offered prayers and burned incense for the Empire's success and safety, and they took their oaths as senators and pledged allegiance to the new emperor at the Altar of Victory. The statue of Victoria on this altar served the function of connecting the Roman state to Rome's religious traditions of various pagan gods and was a symbol of Rome itself and its military supremacy.[1]

And there the statue remained for almost four centuries until 382 CE when Rome's Emperor Gratian ordered the removal of the altar and statue of Victoria. The removal of this ancient altar was a concrete break from the past and a statement about Rome's new religious order. And this created a division in Roman society and in the Roman Senate where the senators were divided. The pagan senators wanted the altar and statue of Victoria to be restored, believing it was part of Rome's history and should remain.[2] The Christian senators wanted it removed, because Rome was now heavily Christian. And so a brewing debate began about the propriety of the pagan altar and statue as symbols of Rome, a debate almost two millennia ago, but a debate that is not fully dissimilar to our debate we just witnessed over the treatment of an American symbol, the flag.

An ancient Roman gold coin in the British Museum produced in 29 BCE - 27 BCE during the reign of Augustus (Octavian). This side illustrates the statue of Victoria as depicted in the original Roman Senate, a winged woman standing on an orb, holding a laurel wreath and palm branch. Copyright the Trustees of the British Museum.

These two factions of senators each wanted the emperor to agree with them, much like we today often have to secure approval from a superior for a business project we want to undertake where there are competing factions seeking approval for their projects. Or we offer our views to a city council meeting on a new city development where others offer contrary views, and the city council will then decide the issue. Not everyone can win as they appeal to the higher authority.

So, the pagan senators decided to approach the emperor with a letter of persuasion to argue for the restoration of the Altar of Victory and statue of Victoria. And to represent them, the pagan senators chose a man called Symmachus, who was considered the greatest orator of his day and a man whom all in Rome respected, pagan or Christian. He came from a pagan family and was also a prefect of Rome. And so Symmachus drafted his argument and sent it to the emperor.[3]

Of his myriad arguments, Symmachus made two arguments that let us explore logical persuasion as he attempted to persuade the emperor to restore the ancient Altar of Victory—a history and tradition argument and a causation argument; both are common arguments we see today in modern persuasion efforts.

1. History and tradition: Symmachus argued that Rome over the centuries thrived and grew with the altar and the attendant ceremonies and social structures that paganism offered. He thus argued that ancient traditions had worked well, and so the gods of Rome should be left unmolested.[4] In essence, Symmachus offered a story about Rome that was rooted in its ancient traditions being important to Rome's thriving and where it was religiously pluralistic, where the new Christian religion could occupy part of that tradition but not supplant it. He ended with a specific, powerful question not unfamiliar to us today, framed in religious tolerance terms, "What

In 384 CE, the emperor decided. Ambrose won. The Altar of Victory and statue of Victoria would not be restored to the Roman Senate. The solid gold statue now is lost to history—although perhaps archaeologists will find it one day—so our understanding of what this magnificent statue looked like comes today from contemporaneous historical descriptions and ancient Roman coins that depicted it.

We now can use our dueling persuaders' competing arguments to unpackage two very important remaining issues of persuasion: first, causation as used in making logical arguments and, second, exaggerated persuasion efforts and how they risk your credibility and the ability to please the audience as well as your ability to prove.

Exaggerating History and Tradition Arguments Is Risky, Because If Not Done Correctly, It Damages Your Credibility and Ability to Prove and Move

Symmachus and Ambrose each offered different versions of history. This is not something relegated to the ancient world. Indeed, it is present in all our lives and persuasive interactions all the time. Almost all of our contentious social issues that divide society involve competing arguments about our history and traditions. For example, people on each side of *Roe v. Wade* point to different aspects of our history to argue for and against protecting the right. When that case and issue was revisited by the Supreme Court, proponents of *Roe v. Wade* pointed to our history of protecting women's rights over their bodies as a key part of the historical tradition we have developed; opponents pointed to the history of allowing states to decide monumental social issues to argue that the matter was for states and not the courts to decide. Two competing visions of history, but only one will prevail. Or as we saw in our flag burning situation, we had competing versions of history and tradition: The flag is a near symbolic part of American history and should be protected versus the history of free speech that should require us to hear things we find deeply hurtful and offensive as expressions of lawful dissent.

This is true at a corporate level too. For example, if a company, say Kodak, has always and successfully made cameras and film, those inside the company who want to move the company into digital products find resistance because status quo proponents point to the century-long history of the company in its space and do not want to change to a new space given the legacy and success of the tradition and history of Kodak in camera film and cameras. On the other side, proponents of pivoting to a new business model argue for the company to drop its ties to that history and focus instead on the history of how the company innovates in the face of technological change and must follow that history when the world changes from analog to digital. With Kodak, we know which side of the internal corporate persuasion debate won, and the winners of their persuasion battle obviously ultimately lost the war for digital camera technology supremacy.

Remember Jackie and Diane. There, too, we saw an accurate use of history by Diane to justify her integral role in our company—she had spent much time working with clients to better the firm and build it—and her need for a raise. Jackie, on the other hand, did not even use a history and tradition argument to contextualize the raise, beyond implying she had been taken advantage of over the prior years due to lower pay.

So, let's pivot back to Symmachus and Ambrose and unpackage their history and tradition arguments to analyze through the persuasion lens why Ambrose offered a better story. Fundamentally, Symmachus's story of Rome's greatness and maintaining its tradition of a multi-religious society—while sounding very powerful when you hear it at first—was based on a foundation that was shaky. That is, he offered a history that was not entirely accurate, and so he reached too far by exaggerating the historical story he told. This enabled Ambrose to prove that Symmachus gave an exaggerated, if not false, account of the facts. Rome had killed Christians, which proved it was not the place of tolerance Symmachus argued for. At that exact moment, Ambrose damaged heavily the credibility of Symmachus because he proved that Symmachus had been false, exaggerated, or dissembled. And those acts damage the speaker's ability to have credibility with an audience. The basic maxim Ambrose offered was this: If one lies about one thing, how can they be trusted in everything else? This is a basic persuasion principle that existed in the ancient world (under the phrase *falsus in uno falsus in maximus*, which translates as false in one, false in all), and the very same maxim applies even in our legal system today.[11] It has existed for the millennia because it is a basic precept of credibility that we must be aware of if we are to persuade.

This means that if we want to advance a persuasive effort about the historical past as part of our story-building effort, it better be accurate. Let's go back to Jackie and Diane. What if Diane had given an account of her relationship with our law firm that was exaggerated for effect to self-aggrandize herself? What if she had claimed that she had worked on specific cases to help us and gone above and beyond, but upon researching, we found that she had simply done her job in the moment, and there was nothing novel or unique about her work? We would have, upon researching the events she identified that justified her raise, realized her story was not accurate. And at that point, she would have certainly lost her request for a raise because we would have lost trust in her. And she would also probably have found herself out of a job because that kind of dishonesty makes one not trustable in other aspects of their job.

It is very easy to fall into this trap, too. In professional working environments, we tend to develop our own stories about our jobs and how well we perform, and we often discount the negative issues in our performance and overstate the positive ones. If you do not take an accurate inventory of the true history, then you risk leading with an exaggerated history and damaging your credibility. To avoid this trap, to avoid doing what Symmachus did, you have to be accurate and honest in your history/tradition logic. Symmachus failed because he overstated the case; Ambrose succeeded because he captured an honest account of the history. If these aspects of logic are to be used, take a very accurate inventory of the facts and do not risk damaging your credibility (ability to please) and logic (ability to prove) by being called out with bad logic.

Faulty Causation Damages Your Logic and Ability to Prove

Causation is a cousin of history and tradition in terms of being another tool of logic. Causation is where one event actually triggers another and is a large part of logical arguments.

Symmachus built his argument in part on his idea of causation to logically prove that the altar should be restored because when it was present, Rome thrived and defeated its enemy Hannibal, and when it was absent, Rome suffered famines. If true, that is a very powerful argument—the same way that if you can show your employer that your sales pitch, in fact, landed the client, then that is a powerful way to prove you caused the new client/revenue to enter your business. But Symmachus got the causation facts wrong, as Ambrose demonstrated. Ambrose demonstrated that famines had occurred when the altar was present in many prior years, proving that the altar's presence did not ward off famines, and he demonstrated that even though a famine occurred after the altar's removal, it was localized, and other parts of the Roman Empire thrived in their crops. That immediately destroyed the logic of Symmachus's causation argument. The causation tool of logic was thus employed in a bad manner and failed.

employees to work remotely at all times, and did not give three weeks of vacation time like our firm. Jackie's claim that the data was comparable and should cause us to match turned out to be wrong.

Persuasion Tools Distilled from the Altar of Victory Story

In our modern world, we often find ourselves in the identical structural system Symmachus and Ambrose found themselves in—a situation where we are offering a vision of something to achieve an end, and someone else is offering a competing vision, and only one will win. A business may be hiring new IT consultants, and your IT company has to offer the best case when a competitor is offering their best case to the hiring business. Or a corporate executive will decide between your team's project idea and another team's project idea, to decide which is best for the company where only one can win.

There are two powerful tools of logic that can be used to prove a moving story: history/tradition and causation. The power of both often yields overuse of them, such that the attempt to prove your point backfires. We thus explored the specific questions to ask yourself to ensure that your causation points are accurate and that your history/tradition points are also accurate.

In each instance, when employing these tools of persuasion, you must persuade by a careful story of history/tradition and accurate causation so that you can please, prove, and then move the decision-maker to your viewpoint.

And how you employ these tools in an extremely heated environment brings us to our last profile in persuasion where we now fast forward in time from Ancient Rome to the Cold War.

Key Takeaways

- When using causation to tell a story and prove, be accurate that there is a proper connection between the two events. Two events may be correlated, but one may not have caused the other.
- When using history and tradition points to tell a story and prove, think carefully about your asserted facts so that you do not offer statements that can be proven wrong.
- Faulty logic damages not only your ability to prove but also your perceived candor and honesty, thereby impacting your credibility to please.

CHAPTER 5

Take the High Road: Cold War Persecution by Prosecution

"Don't raise your voice; improve your argument."

—Desmond Tutu, Speech in South Africa at the Nelson Mandela Foundation, 2004

The Red Scare

Our final profile in persuasion story takes us back to the Great Depression, the Red Scare of Communism, and a time when revolution hung in the air. It begins on the waterfront docks at the Embarcadero in San Francisco in 1934.

Harry Bridges, an Australian immigrant and a working longshoreman, was suffering and seeing the plight of fellow longshoremen on the San Francisco docks. Workers were required to work eighteen-, twenty-four-, and even thirty-six-hour shifts to rapidly offload cargo. If they stopped working, they would be replaced. If they were injured, they were cast aside and on their own. Some men dropped dead while working, and their bodies were left for hours. Attempts to create real unions had failed because the ostensible leaders of the union really had backroom deals with

wrote, "The record in this case will stand forever as a monument to man's intolerance of man. Seldom if ever in the history of this nation has there been such a concentrated and relentless crusade to deport an individual because he dared to exercise the freedom that belongs to him as a human being and that is guaranteed to him by the Constitution."[5]

That crusade, however, continued with aggressive government lawyering. After Bridges won that second trial, he swore in as a citizen. The government then charged him with perjury in his citizenship oath where he had been required to affirm he was not a Communist Party member. If it seems circular, it is; the law's grip, it turns out, can still well perform William Shakespeare's words from *The Merchant of Venice*, "The law hath yet another hold on you." So began a third criminal trial to imprison Bridges for alleged perjury in his citizenship oath. This third trial began in 1949 in San Francisco, a trial that at the time was the longest criminal trial in San Francisco's history.

Bridges' lawyers from his second trial, meanwhile, had been imprisoned for alleged contempt of court for their aggressive representation of other alleged communists. Thus, for his third trial, he hired Vincent Hallinan, a well-known, aggressive lawyer. In that third trial, the government lawyers would not let Hallinan make his opening statement, objecting to almost everything he said. Hallinan refused to stop his opening argument, and by the time of the first witness, the judge held Hallinan in criminal contempt and ordered him to prison.[6]

Pandemonium broke out. United States Marshals grabbed Hallinan's arms to drag him from the court, but Hallinan held onto the podium and charged the judge with a court filing of bias, to which the judge told him, "You will not file any affidavit before me, Mr. Vincent Hallinan." The government lawyers then leapt up and called Hallinan a "mad dog."[7]

The government lawyers then charged Hallinan with turning the court into a brothel. "Mr. Hallinan—I will not refer to him as counsel—I will not prostitute the word by using it in relation to this matter. He has desecrated this temple of justice. ... Your Honor, this is a temple of justice. He is trying to make it a bawdy house."[8]

Because Bridges' other lawyers were already in jail, itself remarkable, the judge allowed Hallinan to continue in the trial. The trial was a long fight with months of acrimony, where at one point Hallinan said of the government prosecutor, "I have not seen inferior merits or inferior qualities better rewarded since Caligula made a consul of his horse and Charles II knighted a beefsteak. ... And I say now in closing that anything I have said about [the prosecutor], any implications or any inferences that I have made to his dishonesty and his corruption, I double and redouble!"[9]

In the end, the jury convicted Bridges in 1950. Hallinan was immediately sent to prison by the judge and spent six months in a federal prison in freezing Puget Sound. But after years of appeals, the Supreme Court in 1953 again reversed Bridges' criminal conviction, finding it baseless (Hallinan, in contrast, served his term).[10]

This brings us to the fourth trial where the government now in 1955 tried a civil denaturalization charge (proving Shakespeare was indeed prescient!). Given the law's vicissitudes and despite the now ten-year-old admonition from Supreme Court Justice Murphy that this was a crusade, this fourth trial was permitted, despite Bridges now winning three times on the question of whether he was a Communist Party member. For this fourth trial, given the circumstances and his prior lawyers' being thrown in jail constantly, Bridges secured yet another lawyer.

This time Bridges hired Telford Taylor, who had been a brigadier general in the United States Army during World War II. At the end of the war, he was one of the lead prosecutors who tried the captured Nazis for their crimes against humanity in the Nuremberg Trials.[11]

Telford Taylor prosecuting the Nazi war criminals after World War II, 1946. Public domain from the United States government.

The Red Scare was at its peak in the early 1950s. Senator Joseph McCarthy had held his famed Senate hearings about the alleged presence of communists next to the House Un-American Activities Committee (HUAC) that held its hearings into the same issue. Thousands of people were decried as communists, their lives and careers ruined by the broader social and political fear environment. Myriad other Americans outed their friends and neighbors so as to secure their personal safety and security in that fear environment. It was indeed a time of fear and retribution, of aggression and destruction, and of change and challenge. And in court, the lawyers, as we have seen, were attacked and even imprisoned, surveilled by the government and even put on government lists.

But Telford Taylor was a lawyer who stood up in that environment and represented that time's most unpopular clients, these alleged communists. He suffered for it, too. Senator McCarthy publicly questioned whether Telford Taylor was a disloyal American.[12]

So, let's explore how Telford Taylor approached this final battle for Harry Bridges. Did he behave like the defense lawyers before him, going blow for blow with the government lawyers in nasty back-and-forth acrimony? Or did he take the high road and stay calm and focused? Did it matter?

Telford Taylor Versus the American Government

As the fourth trial opened, the government prosecutors again went for the kill. As in the prior trials, the government used a new set of witnesses to claim Bridges was a Communist Party member. One witness named Schomaker took the stand in 1955 and testified how he had met Harry Bridges in 1933 and collected Communist Party dues from him. He explained that Bridges pulled out three silver dollars, cocked his head to the right and smirked, and handed over the money.[13]

Taylor had a choice when it came to his chance on cross-examination. He could use his cross-examination to persuade the judge that Schomaker's story was absurd by aggressively challenging the claim of such a minute memory thirty years ago, by calling the

Then, in one of history's most moving persuasion pleas for the calm, steady hand of the law to triumph over a moment of fear, Telford Taylor spoke:

"I would suggest that there are few things as truly important today and that is the law shall remain the law in this country and in all courts wherever they sit, and I am aware your honor is deeply aware of that as anyone here and it would be presumptuous of me to say much more than I have now said. I myself had some opportunity to see in Germany the remains of a society, in which the judges failed the courts, a society in which the judges wrote opinions and became glued to the path of least resistance. And I will conclude by saying to your honor that a judgment for [Harry Bridges] in this case will not be in the deepest sense a judgment against the government, or a judgment for Mr. Bridges or a judgment for or against anybody touched by this controversy. It will be a judgment that the law abides here and that's all the justification it will need."[15]

Let's analyze this high-road approach, and let's not forget the context and temptation Taylor confronted. The Supreme Court had labeled this a crusade, the government had four trials, each with a different set of witnesses, all of whom were found to be perjurers. The temptation to fight and charge the government with corruption—given that history—must have been great, as it was true, but the lawyers in the prior cases tried that tack, and Bridges was repeatedly convicted or ordered deported and imprisoned by the judges and juries.

Taylor thus had to decide how to best persuade. What tools of persuasion to use, what not to do? In this fourth trial, the government had again exaggerated the stakes. And Taylor chose a different path, the high road. Taylor asked more basic questions of the judge, given the facts of the case, questions about simply following the law, ignoring all the drama and hysteria over communism, and instead asking the court to stay focused on due process, not on exaggerations.

Taylor was then able to explain that the government lawyers' aggressive press was really damaging the law more than any one individual, and that should concern any court lest the court go down the road the German courts of the 1930s went down. This also enabled Taylor to tell a different story—one akin to the collapse of German democracy when it caved to its society's fears and exaggerations.

Harry Bridges and Telford Taylor working on Harry Bridges' defense, 1955. Copyright San Francisco History Center, San Francisco Public Library.

And his persuasion story allowed the court to not have to see the case as good versus evil, America versus Harry Bridges; instead, Taylor really made the case about a narrower issue of due process of law: Will a court in a fourth attempt to destroy a man in a twenty-year crusade cave to the time's Red Scare, or will a judge stoically apply due process of law? Will it be a fight between who is corrupt: government or Bridges? Or will be it a fight about the narrow facts only? Does it advance the persuasion effort to make negative accusations back against the government lawyers, or is it better to avoid negative name calling? Taylor answered those questions by taking the high road in his final words, "And I will conclude by saying to Your Honor that a judgment for [Harry Bridges] in this case will not in the deepest sense be a judgment against the government, or a judgment for Mr. Bridges or a judgment for or against anybody touched by this controversy. *It will be a judgment that the law abides here and that's all the justification it will need.*"[16]

The judge agreed with Taylor's narrow approach, rejected the government's broader, more aggressive approach, and Bridges won.[17] The outset question before the subheading of this section asked if it even mattered which tack Taylor took in his persuasion effort—high road or negative acrimony—given the stakes and the government's awesome power to go after Harry Bridges. It did, as we can now see.

Why Negativity Damages Your Credibility

Today, we can unpackage this critical lesson of taking the high road—of not raising your voice and engaging in angry tirades as the chapter's outset quote notes—and not engaging in reciprocal negativity in persuasion terms. First, negative character attacks on people rather than the issues almost always fail because they damage the speaker's credibility. Taking the high road is more effective to persuade people: It allows you to keep your credibility when you want to discuss the specifics—for example, in politics, when you want to explain how the social or economic policies of one side are bad or wrong.

Casting negative aspersions on someone else's character rather than taking the high road is immensely damaging to your ability to persuade. As we discussed earlier, this is known in formal persuasion terms as using an "ad hominem" (Latin for "aimed at the man") at someone as a means of attacking their character rather than their argument. It fails root logic, because it creates the logical fallacy that a message/position is wrong, not on the merits but because of the speaker. "Bad" people can be right on an argument after all; and "good" people can be wrong on an argument—and who is good or bad is often in the eye of the beholder. This kind of negativity is employed to distract, but if you employ it, you damage your persuasive ability to prove with logic because you are now attacking the person rather than what they are saying.

Science in the realm of persuasion has also established this cardinal rule of persuasion. Researchers have blind studied this issue, and in one important study, participants were given multiple versions of the same news article making an argument that a beloved television show should not be canceled; the only difference was the level of anger/negativity used to discuss the argument. Researchers found that the version that was angrier was deemed by viewers as being less trustworthy, the author less competent.[18] That is, in our terms, the negative, angry author lacked credibility on the actual merits of the position being articulated (the core position was the same in each version of the article). This of course comports with the basic principles of persuasion that stand from Cicero's quote at our outset through our profile stories here. After all, you are not always in your own echo chamber where calls to anger may appeal to like-minded, pro-attitudinal people. Rather, in our daily persuasion efforts, we are routinely dealing with people who may hold different viewpoints; hence, we need tools to persuade. The

compelling high-road story Diane developed. For all we know, Diane felt the same as Jackie; perhaps she felt ripped off. But Diane, as with Bono in our opening profile in persuasion and Taylor in this final profile in persuasion, employed words with positive vibrations, spoke with dignity and clarity, and did not set up a story that hinged on good versus bad, her versus us. In so doing, Diane persuaded just as the renowned lawyer Telford Taylor did.

Key Takeaways

- Anger and negativity damage your ability to persuade. The audience perceives you as less trustworthy and accurate, and thereby disengages from your message.
- Attacking the character of your opponent causes you to fall into a logical fallacy trap and damages your ability to persuade. Focus on the story and arguments, not the character of your counterparty.
- Words with negative vibrations can be subtle, so in assessing your chosen story, make sure it does not subtly serve as a character attack on those you are opposed to in your persuasion exercise.

Conclusion

"You don't have to be a fantastic hero to do certain things—to compete. You can be just an ordinary chap, sufficiently motivated to reach challenging goals."

—Edmund Hillary, First with Sherpa Tenzing Norgay to Summit Mount Everest, 1953

Less than a year after President Kennedy's assassination in November 1963, the Democratic Party held its convention for the 1964 election in August in Atlantic City. President Kennedy's brother, Robert F. Kennedy, walked up to the podium on the convention floor. The Democratic party needed unity; should Democrats offer full support for President Lyndon B. Johnson? Did President Kennedy's heir apparent truly support Johnson for reelection?

Before he could speak, the crowd spent a full sixteen minutes cheering him. After the rapturous, emotional applause finally abated, Robert Kennedy spoke, at times haltingly and softly, of a story about the Democratic Party's history of achievements that sustained his brother. He tied that story to the legacy of his slain brother.

"He used to take great pride in telling of the trip that Thomas Jefferson and James Madison made up the Hudson River in 1800 on a botanical expedition searching for butterflies; that they ended up down in New York City and that they formed the Democratic Party. He took great pride in the fact that the Democratic Party was the oldest political Party in the world .... He thought of Thomas Jefferson in the Louisiana Purchase, and also when Jefferson realized that the United States could not remain on the Eastern Seaboard and sent Lewis and Clark to the West Coast; of Andrew Jackson; of Woodrow Wilson; of Franklin Roosevelt who saved our citizens who were in great despair because of the financial crisis; of Harry Truman who not only spoke but acted for freedom. ... So I join with you in realizing that what started four years ago—what everyone here started four years ago—that is to be sustained; that is to be continued. The same effort and the same energy and the same dedication that was given to President John F. Kennedy must be given to President Lyndon Johnson and Hubert Humphrey," Robert Kennedy offered as a story.[1]

Robert F. Kennedy speaking at the Democratic National Convention on August 27, 1964, where he gave his speech as a tribute to President John F. Kennedy. Photographer Steve Schapiro, Copyright Getty.

Robert Kennedy's brief nine-minute speech used a universal story structure, one similar to the types of stories that demonstrate proper responses in listeners as detailed by Dr. Zak in his studies we discussed. Indeed, Robert Kennedy's short speech could have had its own chapter here as a profile in persuasion.[2] But for our purposes, what matters about Robert Kennedy's words is *how* he delivered them. Robert Kennedy was not then the soaring orator that President Kennedy had been, nor did he deliver that speech with the more traditional oratorical flare that he used in later years such as the

tools to their persuasion efforts to secure our votes or agreement itself allows us to better unpackage the truth of the competing claims we have to analyze to make our voting and social policy decisions. Are our politicians speaking with credibility and authenticity? Are they overstating their case with exaggerated claims that let us question their sincerity? Are they treating us, the voters (their audience), with respect, and do they speak to their opponents with respect? Or do they make hyperbolic claims that are not credible? The tools of persuasion can help us unpackage the volume of data we are receiving, separate the noise of the situation from the true facts, and at least make informed decisions about who is the more credible persuader, who is the better storyteller. And in so doing, we can then better understand how to stand up and persuade for ourselves and our families and communities.

U2's Bono, President John F. Kennedy, Attorneys William Kunstler and Telford Taylor, and Bishop Ambrose are spread across the arc of time, place, and societies. They all breathed different air, lived in drastically different societies, and confronted very different challenges. But they all masterfully practiced persuasion. In so doing, they all stood up for their beliefs and causes as they faced overwhelming odds and adversity to prevail in their persuasion efforts. But they all in fact prevailed in their persuasion. They all persuaded with powerful stories that properly used the tools of persuasion. As a result, they moved adverse audiences to secure AIDS relief that has saved millions of lives, moved an audience to achieve the impossible and go to the Moon within a decade, secured First Amendment freedoms to express dissent, ended a twenty-year campaign of persecution by prosecution, and altered hundreds of years of history in the ancient Roman Senate. But in their persuasion efforts, they did not cave to the elixir of negativity. They persuaded with calm and respectful words, without venom and bitterness, without recrimination and personal attacks, and with words whose vibrations have echoed for decades and even millennia. They used the tools of persuasion. They pleased, they proved, and they moved. So can we all.

The Persuasion Please/ Prove/Move Toolbox (One-on-One, One-on-Many, One-Versus-One)

Please Tools	Prove Tools	Move Tools
Credibility—the proper basis to say what you are saying	Story structure with story elements—carefully and intentionally chosen to avoid negative consequences of a story that at first blush may sound appealing but may instead boomerang on you	Story structure with story elements—carefully and intentionally chosen to avoid negative consequences of a story that at first blush may sound appealing but may instead boomerang on you
Authenticity—be the best version of yourself and do not adopt another persona (improve your lane; do not change lanes!)	Metaphors	Metaphors

Endnotes

Introduction

1. Marcus Tullius Cicero, *On the Ideal Orator* (*De Oratore*), translated by James M. May and Jakob Wisse, p. 207 (Book 2: 306-10) (Oxford University Press 2001).
2. Marcus Tullius Cicero, *Cicero in 28 Volumes* (*De Optimo Genere Oratorum*), translated by H. M. Hubbell, p. 357 (Book 1:1.3) (Harvard University Press 1949).

Chapter 1

1. Chuck Smith, "The Case Against Jesse Helms," *Wall Street Journal* (Sep. 4, 2001).
2. "Filibuster by Helms on Dr. King Holiday Is Dropped in Senate," *New York Times* (Oct. 5, 1983).
3. Edward I. Koch, "Senator Helms' Callousness Towards ADIS Victims," *New York Times* (Nov. 7, 1987); "AIDS Booklet Stirs Senate to Halt Funds," *Los Angeles Times* (Oct. 14, 1987) (Helms says on the Senate floor of homosexuality, "This subject matter is so obscene, so revolting, it is difficult for me to stand here and talk about it.... I may throw up.").

4. Ellen McGirt, "Bono: I Will Follow," *Fortune Magazine* (Mar. 24, 2016).
5. *See, e.g.,* Bono, *Surrender*, p. 399 (Penguin Random House 2002); "U2 Members Fretted Over Bono's Activism," *Associated Press* (Jan. 27, 2006), located at https://www.foxnews.com/story/u2-members-fretted-over-bonos-activism.amp (last accessed Jan. 5, 2025); Dorian Lynskey, "Ego Warriors: U2 Speaks Out on Rock-Star Hypocrisy," *The Guardian* (July 30, 2009) (reporting the band's manager told Bono the rock star should describe problems, not fix them).
6. Paul Brannigan, "How Bono and the Edge's Faith in Jesus Almost Destroyed U2," *Louder* (June 12, 2025) located at https://www.loudersound.com/bands-artists/how-jesus-almost-destroyed-u2 (last accessed Sep. 23, 2025); David Evans ("The Edge"), "Gloria," *U2 The Complete Lyrics 1979-1988 Volume I*, p.34 (U2 Limited, 2023) ("At the same time, we were trying to square the circle of faith of rock 'n' roll and how all that worked. There was a period where it was so difficult for us to reconcile the two…").
7. U2, "Where the Streets Have No Name," Boston Live Concert, 2001, timestamp :19-1:28 located at https://www.youtube.com/watch?v=AjeuNxRKKts.
8. *Supra* McGirt, "Bono: I Will Follow."
9. Matthew 25:31-46 (New American Standard Bible); *ibid.* 25:35-36 ("For I was hungry, and you gave Me something to eat; I was thirsty, and you gave Me something to drink; I was a stranger, and you invited Me in; naked, and you clothed Me; I was sick, and you visited Me; I was in prison, and you came to Me.").
10. Bill Frist, "How a Rock-Star, a Physician-Legislator, and an Evangelical Senator Bonded to Help End the Global AIDS Pandemic: A Backstory," *Forbes Magazine* (Dec. 1, 2022).
11. Bono, *Surrender*, p. 399.

12. *Supra* McGirt, "Bono: I Will Follow."
13. Bono, *Surrender,* p. 399.
14. Adam Clymer, "Helms Reverses Opposition to Help on AIDS," *New York Times* (Mar. 26, 2002).
15. *Supra,* Frist, "How a Rock Star…"
16. *Supra,* McGirt, "Bono: I Will Follow."
17. Global Health Security and Diplomacy, United States Department of State, "PEPFAR Latest Global Results & Projections," United States State Department (December 1, 2024); Eric A. Friedman, Sarah A. Wetter, and Lawrence O. Gostin, "PEPFAR Funding to Fight HIV/AIDS Has Saved 26 Million Lives Since 2003: How Cutting It Will Hurt Africa," *The Conversation* (March 4, 2025), located at https://theconversation.com/pepfar-funding-to-fight-hiv-aids-has-saved-26-million-lives-since-2003-how-cutting-it-will-hurt-africa-250413#:~:text=The%20investment%20of%20over%20US,from%20being%20born%20with%20HIV (last accessed Sep. 23, 2025).
18. *Supra* fn. 3, 1.
19. Stefan Rozental (editor), *Niels Bohr: His Life and Work as Seen by His Friends and Colleagues,* (Elsevier Science Limited 1985), p. 328; Michael Guillen, "The Deepest Truths Are Not Logical. That Includes God," Substack (Sep. 7, 2025) (paraphrasing Niels Bohr from the prior referenced book); Max Delbrück, *Mind from Matter: An Essay on Evolutionary Epistemology,* (Blackwell Scientific Publications 1986), p. 167.

Chapter 2

1. President John F. Kennedy, *Special Message to Congress on Urgent Needs* (May 25, 1961).
2. John M. Logsdon, *John F. Kennedy and the Race to the Moon* (Palgrave Macmillan 2011); Alexis C. Madrigal,

17. *Id.* at 11:21-12:1.
18. *Id.* at 12:2-7.
19. *Id.* at 44:3-49:7.
20. *Texas v. Johnson*, 491 U.S. at 405.
21. *Texas v. Johnson*, 491 U.S. at 409.
22. *Texas v. Johnson*, 491 U.S. at 414.
23. *United States v. Eichman*, 496 U.S. 310 (1990).
24. Flag Protection Act of 1989, 103 Stat. 777, codified at 77 U.S.C. § 700.
25. *Texas v. Johnson* Oral Argument Official Transcript, March 21, 1989, at 38:9-11.
26. *Id.* at 38:12-18.
27. Goldstein, *Flag Burning & Free Speech*, at 95-96.
28. *United States v. Eichman* Oral Argument Official Transcript, May 14, 1990, at 24:15-25:9.
29. Robert B. Cialdini, *Influence: The Psychology of Persuasion* (Harper Business 2021).
30. *Eichman*, 496 U.S. at 317 ("Although Congress cast the Flag Protection Act in somewhat broader terms than the Texas statute at issue in *Johnson*, the Act still suffers from the same fundamental flaw: it suppresses expression out of concern for its likely communicative impact.").

Chapter 4

1. James J. Sheridan, "The Altar of Victory—Paganism's Last Battle," *L'antique Classique* (1966), at 186-88; Mattias P. Gassman, *Worshippers of the Gods: Debating Paganism in the Fourth-Century Roman West*, (Oxford Univ. Press 2020), p. 107-09.
2. *Id.*
3. *Id.* at 194; Gassman, *Worshippers of the Gods*, at 110.
4. *Id.* at 200; Gassman, *Worshippers of the Gods*, at 117.
5. Gassman, *Worshippers of the Gods*, at 117, 124.

6. *Id.* at 203.
7. *Id.* at 194.
8. *Id.* at 200-01; Gassman, *Worshippers of the Gods*, at 117, 134.
9. Gassman, *Worshippers of the Gods*, p. 134.
10. *Id.* at 203-04.
11. *See, e.g.*, California Civil Jury Instruction 107 (2025) ("… if you decide that a witness did not tell the truth about something important, you may choose not to believe anything that witness said.").

Chapter 5

1. Peter Afrasiabi, *Burning Bridges: America's 20-Year Crusade to Deport Labor Leader Harry Bridges* (Thirlmere Books 2017), p. 3-22.
2. *Id.* at 22-61.
3. *Id.* at 103-15.
4. *Id.* at 125.
5. *Bridges v. Wixon*, 326 U.S. 135, 157 (1945).
6. Afrasiabi, *Burning Bridges*, p. 156-72.
7. *Id.* at 172.
8. *Id.* at 173.
9. *Id.* at 181.
10. *Bridges v. United States*, 346 U.S. 208 (1953).
11. Afrasiabi, *Burning Bridges*, p. 203-15.
12. "McCarthy Says West Point Critic has 'Unresolved' Loyalty Record," *New York Times* (Dec. 1, 1953).
13. Afrasiabi, *Burning Bridges*, p. 217-20.
14. *Id.*
15. *United States v. Harry Bridges*, Case No. 28876, Closing Arguments, July 21, 1955, p. 1879-80.
16. *Id.*
17. *United States v. Bridges*, 133 F. Supp. 638, 643 (N.D. Cal. 1955) ("Only a weak yielding to extra-judicial clamor would

excuse acceptance of the testimony of the witnesses in this case as proof of the allegations of the complaint.").

18. Jonathan Van't Riet, Gabi Schaap & Mariska Kleemans, "Fret not thyself: The persuasive effect of anger expression and the role of perceived appropriateness," *Motivation and Emotion* (December 8, 2017), located at https://link.springer.com/article/10.1007/s11031-017-9661-3 (last accessed Sep. 23, 2025); *see also* Deborah Small & Jennifer Lerner, "Emotional Policy: Personal Sadness and Anger Shape Judgments About a Welfare Case," *Political Psychology* Vol. 29, No. 2 (2008). Some studies also show that the use of moderate anger can motivate people already in line with a viewpoint (pro-attitudinal people) to agree if there is an avenue to direct the anger into the listener's already-existing preferred state. *See* Nathan Walter et al., "Meta-Analysis of Anger and Persuasion: An Empirical Integration of Four Models," Chapman University, Communication Faculty Articles and Research (October 27, 2018). For persuasion in our daily lives, however, the use of anger to persuade those not already fully in line with our views (hence those people not needed even to be "persuaded" in our terms here) remains risky to basic precepts of persuasion. And these lessons in persuasion are decidedly focused on everyday life's use of persuasion, not, for example, on specific advocacy groups speaking to their base to raise money for a cause.
19. Honorable Amy St. Eve and Gretchen Scavo, "What Juries *Really* Think: Practical Guidance for Trial Lawyers," Cornell Law Review Volume 103:149 (2018) (In studies, among the things jurors like least is negative behavior and unprofessional conduct, as well as a lack of brevity).

Conclusion

1. Papers of Robert F. Kennedy, Attorney General Papers, Box 255, "1964: 8/27, Introduction to *A Thousand Days*, Democratic National Convention, Atlantic City, NJ, 9pp. [Tribute to John F. Kennedy]: Final Draft & Text of Remarks," John F. Kennedy Presidential Library. Available at: https://www.jfklibrary.org/learn/about-jfk/the-kennedy-family/robert-f-kennedy/robert-f-kennedy-speeches/tribute-to-john-f-kennedy-at-the-democratic-national-convention-atlantic-city-new-jersey-august-27 (last accessed Sep. 23, 2025).
2. His speech had a central story (the Democratic Party's history as viewed by his brother), characters (President Kennedy, the Party and, on the other side, those who doubted Lyndon Johnson), and a point of contention that led to the climactic resolution (support Lyndon Johnson to continue President Kennedy's legacy). He also used powerful word rhythms, as he delivered his story that contextualized President Kennedy's achievements as part of a relevant tradition. The speech's brilliance lands on many other levels also, including the politics of the situation, the need to support Johnson but cement his brother's legacy, and the need to leave the door open for Robert Kennedy to challenge Johnson down the road.
3. You can listen to the speech here: https://www.c-span.org/program/american-history-tv/robert-kennedy-1964-convention-speech/193767.

About the Author

Peter Afrasiabi has taught advocacy and persuasion at major American universities, the National Institute for Trial Advocacy, and to barristers at training programs held at Oxford University in the UK. He is the host of a national education series, *The Curious Lawyer*, teaching persuasion techniques and legal education programs; has been interviewed and appeared on major national news and media outlets; and has a US patent on software to help online personal persuasion efforts. As a lawyer, Peter has advocated in federal and state courts from California to New York to DC; in significant copyright, IP, and business disputes; as well as in civil rights and immigration cases of significant national import all the way to the Supreme Court.

Peter has spent a quarter century both practicing advocacy professionally and teaching it, and in this book, he converts the hard-learned lessons of professional persuasion into easy-to-understand-and-master tools that all of us can and must practice, all by engaging with fun, exciting stories. Peter's last book, *Burning Bridges*, was an Amazon Top Seller and detailed the serial trials of labor leader Harry Bridges during the Cold War.